C++

Step by step Beginners Guide in Mastering C++

Liam Damien

© Copyright 2019 - Liam Damien - All rights reserved.

This document is geared towards providing exact and reliable information in regard to the topic and issue covered. The publication is sold with the idea that the publisher is not required to render accounting, officially permitted, or otherwise, qualified services. If advice is necessary, legal or professional, a practiced individual in the profession should be ordered.

- From a Declaration of Principles which was accepted and approved equally by a Committee of the American Bar Association and a Committee of Publishers and Associations.

In no way is it legal to reproduce, duplicate, or transmit any part of this document in either electronic means or in printed format. Recording of this publication is strictly prohibited and any storage of this document is not allowed unless with written permission from the publisher. All rights reserved.

The information provided herein is stated to be truthful and consistent, in that any liability, in terms of inattention or otherwise, by any usage or abuse of any policies, processes, or directions contained within is the solitary and utter responsibility of the recipient reader. Under no circumstances will any legal responsibility or blame be held against the publisher for any reparation, damages, or monetary loss due to the information herein, either directly or indirectly.

Respective authors own all copyrights not held by the publisher.

The information herein is offered for informational purposes solely and is universal as so. The presentation of the information is without contract or any type of guarantee assurance.

The trademarks that are used are without any consent, and the publication of the trademark is without permission or backing by the trademark owner. All trademarks and brands within this book are for clarifying purposes only and are the owned by the owners themselves, not affiliated with this document.

Table of Contents

Preface 1

Chapter 1: Introduction to C++ Programming Language 2

    1.2: Programming Techniques 3

        1.2.1: Structured Programming 3

        1.2.2: Object-Oriented Programming (OOP) 7

        1.2.3: Event-Driven Programming (EDP) 8

        1.2.4: Visual Programming 8

    1.3: Features of C++ 8

    1.4: Basic Structure of the C++ Program 9

    1.5: Creating a C++ Program 11

    1.6: Debugging a C++ Program 12

        1.6.1: Types of Errors 13

Chapter 2: Programming With C++ 15

    2.1: Identifier 15

        2.1.1: Types of Identifiers 16

    2.2: Keywords 16

    2.3: Datatypes 18

        2.3.1: Integer Datatype 19

        2.3.2: Float Datatype 20

2.3.3: Double Datatype 20

2.3.4: Char Datatype: 21

2.4: Variables 21

    2.4.1: Variable Declaration 22

    2.4.2: Rules for Variable Declaration 22

    2.4.3: Variable Initialization 23

    2.4.4: Variable Scope 24

2.5: Constants 25

    2.5.1: Literal Constants 25

    2.5.2: Symbolic Constants 26

2.6: Expression 27

2.7: Operators 27

    2.7.1: Unary Operator 27

    2.7.2: Binary Operators 28

    2.7.3: Assignment Statement 29

    2.7.4: Compound Assignment Statement 29

    2.7.5: Compound Assignment Operators 30

    2.7.6: Increment Operator 30

    2.7.7: Decrement Operator 31

    2.7.8: Operator Precedence 32

    2.7.9: Operator Associativity 33

    2.7.10: The "sizeof" Operator 34

2.8: Type Casting 34

2.9: Comments 35

Chapter 3: Input and Output 37

3.1: Standard Input 37

3.2: Standard Output 37

3.3: Escape Sequence 39

3.4: C++ Manipulators 46

Practice Exercise 1 48

Solution Practice Exercise 1 50

Chapter 4: Structures 62

4.1: Control Structure 62

    4.1.1: Types of Control Structures 62

4.2: Relational Operators 63

    4.2.1: Relational Expression 64

4.3: 'if' Statement 65

    4.3.1: Limitations for 'if' Statement 66

4.4: 'if-else' Statement 67

4.6: Nested 'if' Statement 73

4.7: Compound Condition 75

    4.7.1: Logical Operators 75

4.8: Switch Statement 77

4.9: Conditional Operator 80

4.10: 'goto' Statement 81

Practice Exercise 2 82

Chapter 5: Looping Structures 84

5.1: Loops 84

    5.1.1: Counter-Controlled Loops 84

- 5.1.2: Sentinel-Controlled Loops 85
- 5.2: 'while' Loop 85
- 5.3: 'do-while' Loop 89
- 5.4: 'for' Loop 91
  - 5.4.1: 'continue' Statement 92
  - 5.4.2: 'break Statement 94
- 5.5: Nested Loops 95
- Practice Exercise 3 98

Chapter 6: Arrays 104

- 6.1: Introduction to Arrays 104
  - 6.1.1: Declaration of One-Dimensional Array 105
  - 6.1.2: Array Initialization 105
  - 6.1.3: Accessing Individual Elements of Array..................... 106
  - 6.1.4: Accessing the Array Elements using Loops 107
  - 6.1.5: Input and Output Values of an Array 107
- 6.2: Searching in Arrays 111
  - 6.2.1: Sequential Search 111
  - 6.2.2: Binary Search 113
- 6.3: Sorting of Arrays 115
  - 6.3.1 Selection Sort 122
  - 6.3.2: Bubble Sort 125
- 6.4: Two-Dimensional Arrays 127
  - 6.4.1: Accessing Elements of 2-D Array 128
  - 6.4.2: inputting data into a 2-D array 128
  - 6.4.3: Initializing 2-D Arrays 128
- 6.5 Multidimensional Array 130

6.5.1: Accessing Multidimensional Array 130

Practice Exercise 4 132

Chapter 7: Structures 134

7.1.1: Declaring a Structure 134

7.1.2: Defining a Structure Variable 136

7.1.3: Accessing variables of a structure 136

7.1.4: Initializing Structure Variables................................. 138

7.1.5: Assigning one structure to another structure variable 140

7.1.6: Array as a Member of Structure.............................. 142

7.2: Array of Structures 145

7.2.1: Initializing Array of Structures................................. 145

7.3: Nested Structures... 148

7.3.1: Accessing Members of Nested Structure 149

7.4: Unions.. 151

Practice Exercise 5 154

Chapter 8: Functions 155

8.1.1: Advantages of a Function 156

8.2: Types of Functions in C++... 157

8.3: User-Defined Functions 157

8.3.1: Function Declaration or Function Prototyping.......... 157

8.3.2: Function Definition 158

8.3.3: Function Call 159

8.3.4: Scope of Functions 161

8.4: Passing Parameters to Functions 162

8.4.1: Passing Function by Value 162

8.4.2: Passing a Function by Reference 164

8.4.3: Returning a Value from the Function 166

8.5: Functions and Arrays 170

8.5.1: Function Calling with an Array 170

8.5.2: Two-Dimensional Array as a
parameter to a Function 172

8.6: Passing Structure to Functions 175

8.7: Default Parameters 178

8.8: Functions Overloading 179

8.9: Recursion 181

Practice Exercise 6 183

Chapter 9: Built-in Functions in C++ 185

9.1: The Header File 'conio.h' 185

9.2: The Header File 'stdio.h' 188

9.3: The Header File 'ctype.h' 192

Chapter 10: Pointers 194

10.1.1: Declaring a Pointer 194

10.1.2: Initializing a pointer 195

10.2: Operation Performed on Pointers 196

10.3: Pointers with Arrays 197

10.4: An Array of Pointers 198

10.5: Pointers with Functions 200

10.6: Pointers and Memory Management 202

Practice Exercise 6 204

Chapter 11: String Handling 205

- 11.1: String 205
  - 11.1.1: String Declaration 205
  - 11.1.2: String Initialization 206
- 11.2: String Input 206
- 11.3: String Functions Header File (string.h) 210
- Practice Exercise 7 220

Chapter 12: Basics of Object-Oriented Programming 222

- 12.1: Introduction 222
  - 12.1.1: Object-Oriented Programming Features 223
- 12.2: Objects 223
- 12.3: Classes in OOP 224
  - 12.3.1: Declaring a Class in C++ 225
  - 12.3.2: Access Specifiers in Classes 226
- 12.4: Creating Objects in C++ 227
  - 12.4.1: Executing Member Functions of a Class 228
  - 12.4.2: Declaring the Member Functions Outside a Class .. 230
- 12.5: Constructors in Classes 232
  - 12.5.1: Parameters to Constructors 233
  - 12.5.2: Constructor Overloading in Classes 235
- 12.6: Destructors in Classes 236
- 12.7: Friend Classes in OOP 238
- Practice Exercise 8 241

Chapter 13: Inheritance 242

- 13.1: Introduction 242
  - 13.1.1: Advantages of inheritance 243

13.1.2: Types of Inheritance 243

13.2: Declaring a Child Class 244

13.3: Accessing Members and Functions of Parent Class 246

13.4: Types of Inheritance in C++ 250

Practice Exercise 9 253

Chapter 14: File Handling 254

14.1: Introduction to Files 254

14.2: File Access Methods 255

14.3: Stream 256

14.4: Opening and Closing of Files in C++ 258

Short Questions 261

Conclusion 266

References 267

Preface

The main objective of this book" **Step by Step Beginners Guide in Mastering C++** "is to provide complete assistance to the students to get expertise in C++ programming techniques. It helps you to learn not only the basics of the language but also coding and debugging. It covers all the aspects such as, coding, design, editing, debugging and execution of C++ programs.

Developing a good program includes more than just typing the piece of code. Programming is an art in which coding and programming knowledge are integrated to produce a masterpiece. A correct C++ program is not only to define the functions accurately but also it must be simple and easy to understand. Comments on the programming language allow programmers to include the typical description of their programs.

A program written in the C++ programming language should be clearer and more convenient. Avoid using wrong programming tricks and cleverness. Cleverness can kill the purpose of the programs that result in a waste of time only. My aim behind writing this book is to convey the complete knowledge of the C++ programming language to the learners.

Chapter 1

Introduction to C++ Programming Language

C++ is a multi-paradigm programming language developed by a great computer scientist named "Bjarne Stroustrup at A T and T Bells Lab in the 1970's. It was developed as an advancement upon the C language. C language was only designed for Unix operating systems. Then Stroustrup decided to work on the idea of object-oriented programming (OOP) and in the results he developed C++. C++ is a widely used industrial programming language which is used to develop more complex and large-scale industrial systems. Applications of C++ programming are Windows, macOS, Microsoft Office, Adobe utility software, MySQL, C#, Java, Python, Perl, and PHP. (The C++ programming language., (2000))

C++ is close to computer hardware and easy to understand by programmers. It provides a complete knowledge of object-oriented programming. If anyone wanted to become a good developer, C++ programming language is a must to learn to be a good programmer. It is a standardized version of C that was created by ANSI (American National Standards Institute). C++ is the hybrid of both low-level and high-level languages, so it enables programmers to create application software, other programming languages, games, and embedded systems.

1.2: Programming Techniques

There are multiple programming techniques available to write a computer program. These techniques describe the concepts used in computer programming. Some of the programming techniques are:

1.2.1: Structured Programming

In this technique, programs are divided into small subprograms or modules. Each subprogram consists of the instructions to perform specific tasks. Subprograms are executed when the main function calls them. After the execution of subprograms, control moves back to the location where it called the specific module or subprogram.

It's an easy approach to writing computer programs that are easy to read, check and update. To write longer projects, structured programming is further divided into categories that are as follows:

- **Sequential Structure:**

Statements in sequential structure are executed in the sequence in which they are written. The program control flows from one statement to another to execute it. There is no repetition and all statements are executed once. It means that no statement is missed or executed twice.

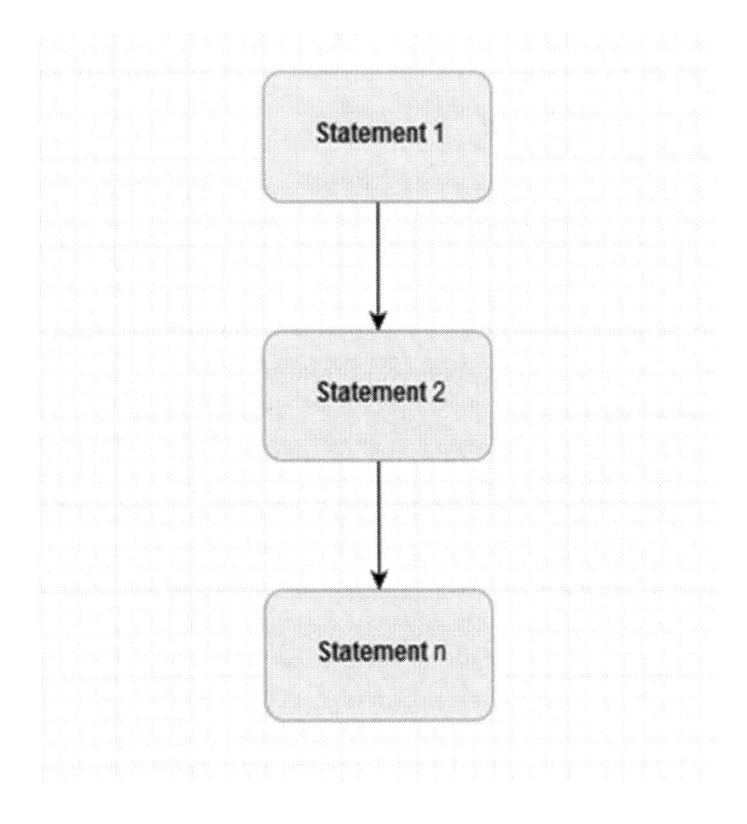

Figure 1.2.1: Sequential Structure

- **Selection Structure:**

The selection structure selects a particular statement or set of statements by checking the given condition. When the condition remains **TRUE,** the specific statement or set of statements are executed but ignored if the condition remains **FALSE**.

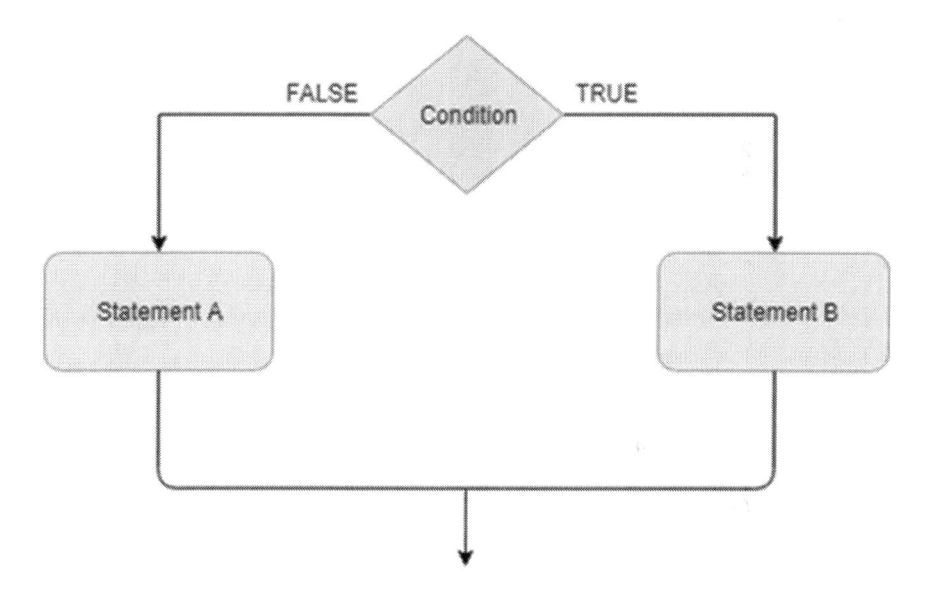

Figure 1.2.1: Selection Structure

- **Iterative Structure:**

In iterative structure, the statement or block of statements are executed until the given condition remains true.

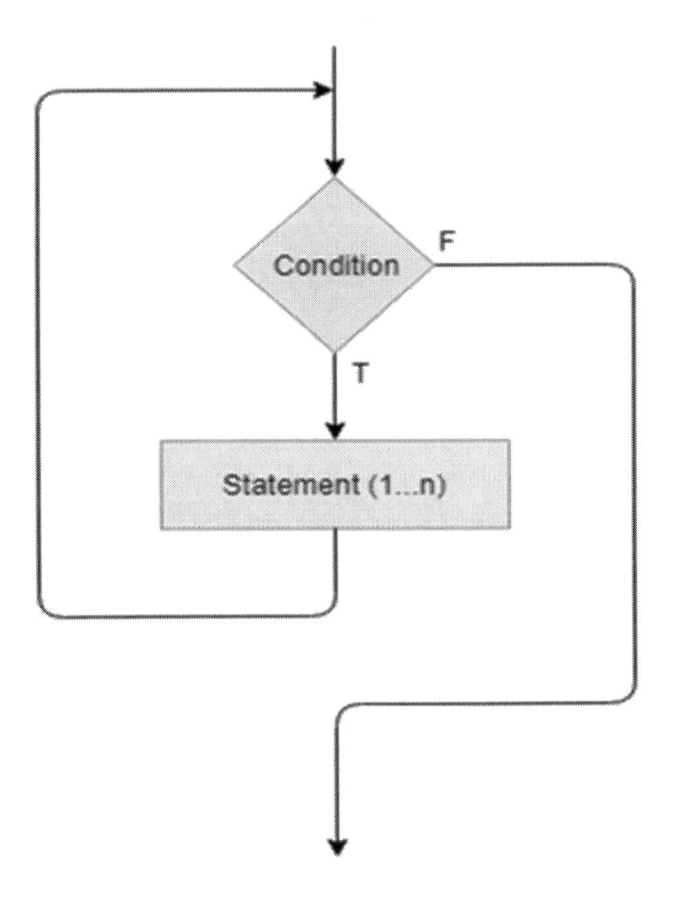

Figure 1.2.1: Iterative Structure

- **Function Call:**

In the function call, control is moved to a specific block of code when it is called. And after executing the particular statements, control moves back to the place from where it was called.

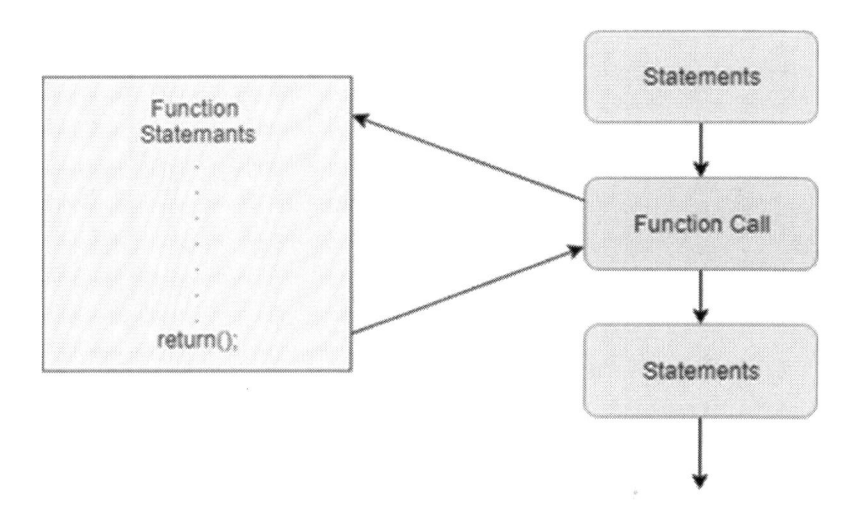

Figure 1.2.1: Function Call Structure

1.2.2: Object-Oriented Programming (OOP)

OOP is an approach of a procedural programming language in which programs are written based on individual objects. Objects are the building blocks of the program and are easy to use and maintain. In object-oriented programming, all the data and the functions performed on that data are grouped. A real-life example of OOP is a person, considered as an object because it has several properties, namely the name, age, height, color, and it has functions, which are walking, talking and eating. (Cox, 1986)

1.2.3: Event-Driven Programming (EDP)

Event-driven programming refers to writing code to perform particular events. An event occurs when some actions are performed. For example:

- The event of clicking the mouse button must have some back-end programming to act as the system.

- Typing from a keyboard.

1.2.4: Visual Programming

This is a programming technique that is used to create a user-friendly interface to interact with computer programs. Different objects, like icons, menus, and buttons, to make a graphical interface. Visual programming includes developing program interfaces by using built-in objects and components. In visual programming, the programmer does not need to code for development. Everything is done by drag and drop. It is easy to use and learn. (Kiczales, 1997, June)

1.3: Features of C++

Important features of C++ programming language are:

- Well-structured language
- Convenient language

- Case sensitive
- Object-oriented
- Machine independent
- Hardware control
- Brevity
- Speed
- Standard libraries

1.4: Basic Structure of the C++ Program

The pattern of writing a program is called a structure. The structure of a C++ program consists of the following three parts:

- **Preprocessor directive:**

These are the instructions that are given to the compiler to get an idea of the what should be in the program body. It starts with a "#" symbol.

An example of preprocessor directives are

#include<stdio.h>   //used for standard input/output stream of data functions.

#include<stdlib.h>   //used for standard libraries used in the program.

- **Main() function:**

It is the starting point of the program from where the program execution begins. The Main() function is a the most important part of a C++ program. If a program does not have a Main() function, execution cannot be started.

An example:

// When the compiler reads the main function the
program execution is started.

Void main()
{
The program body exists here.
}

- **Program body:**

This is the area where the C++ program statements are written, inside the curly brackets. These are the C++ statements that perform the desired task and produce results. Each statement in a C++ program is terminated by a semicolon.

An example:

{

C++ statements here

.

.

.

.

.

.

}

1.5: Creating a C++ Program

The process of creating a C++ program consists of the following steps.

- **Creating or writing the C++ program code:**

To write a program, first of all, we have to open an IDE (Integrated Development Environment); this is an editor where the code or program is written. Some of the IDE's are Turbo C++ and Cfree.

- **Saving a C++ program:**

After creating or writing the program instructions, it is saved in the specific directory named as "**BIN**". All programs will be saved with an extension ".**cpp**".

- **Compiling a C++ program:**

After saving it, a program must be compiled to check for errors. The program saved with the .cpp extension is called a source program. So, we have to convert the source program into an object program before execution. This process is called the compilation of a program.

- **Linking a C++ program:**

As we have used multiple library files in our program, we have to link those library files to the object file before execution. The process of linking the object files with the library files is called the linking of a program.

- **Executing a C++ program:**

To get the output of the program code, we have to run the program after compilation. This process is called the execution of a program. After the execution of the program, the output generated by the program is the code displayed on the screen.

1.6: Debugging a C++ Program

Errors in computer programs are called bugs. The process of searching and removing bugs and errors from the program is referred to as Debugging. In this process, when the compiler compiles the program, it notifies the programmer if the program code has any error. The programmer has to remove all the bugs to make the program work right.

1.6.1: Types of Errors

Several types of errors that occur in C++ programs are logical errors, syntax errors, and run-time errors.

- **Logical Errors:**

Errors that occur due to poor programming logic are called logical errors. This type of error may produce wrong and unexpected results. Logical errors are difficult to be detected by compiler or program translator. The programmer must review the entire program thoroughly to detect logical errors and it can be time-consuming.

- **Syntax Errors:**

Every programming language has its predefined set of rules to write the code or programs. These rules are called the syntax. Logical errors occur due to incorrect syntax or an invalid statement used in the program. The compiler detects the logical errors and displays an error message on the screen with the reference statement. The programmer must eliminate all the syntax errors to compile the program successfully.

- **Run-time Errors:**

A type of error that occurs at the time of program execution is called a run-time error. Run-time errors cannot be detected by the compiler or translator. They are caused when a program asks the computer system to perform an invalid operation, such as dividing a number by 0.

The computer system stops the program execution and shows an error message on the screen if a run-time error is detected.

Chapter 2

Programming With C++

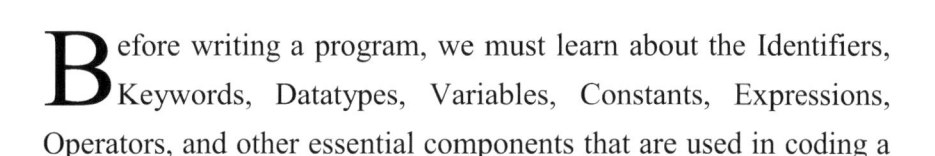

Before writing a program, we must learn about the Identifiers, Keywords, Datatypes, Variables, Constants, Expressions, Operators, and other essential components that are used in coding a program.

2.1: Identifier

Names used to represent the variables, functions, types, constants and the labels are called Identifiers. Identifiers are an important part of computer programs. In C++, an identifier may consist of up to 31 characters. Important rules for defining the identifier are:

- The first letter of the identifier name must be alphabetical (A – Z or a – z) or an underscore (_).

- The identifier name must consist of alphabetical letters, numeric digits, or underscores.

- The identifier name cannot have any reserved keyword.

2.1.1: Types of Identifiers

Types of identifiers provided by C++ are:

- **Standard Identifiers:**

Identifiers that have some special purposes in the C++ programming language are called Standard Identifiers. For example, **cout and cin** are the standard identifiers used for input and output purposes in the C++ programming language.

- **User-Defined Identifiers:**

Identifiers that are defined by the programmers to perform specific tasks are called User-defined identifiers. These identifiers are used for memory access and are stored in the iostream.h library.

2.2: Keywords

Keywords are the reserved words in C++ that have a predefined task, defined by the developer of the language. Keywords cannot be changed or modified by programmers. The keywords and their purposes in C++ are:

Keywords	Purpose
and	Used as an alternative operator.
asm	Used to insert an assembly language.
bool	Used to declare a Boolean operator.

break	Used to get control out from the loop.
case	A block of code used in the Switch statement.
int	Used to declare an integer variable.
char	Used to declare a character variable.
float	Used to declare a float type of variable.
const	Used to make the value constant throughout the program.
class	Used to declare a class in C++.
delete	Used to make the dynamic memory available/free.
else	Alternate case of an if statement.
exit()	Used to end a running process.
goto	used to jump to another part of the program.
if	Used in the conditional statement which produces the result based on a condition.
new	Used to allocate dynamic memory in program execution.
private	Used to declare the private variable in the class.
Sizeof	It returns the size or type of the variable in the memory.
typeid	It is used to describe an object.
union	A type of structure used to assign multiple values to the same memory.
unsigned	Used to declare an unsigned variable.

using	Keyword to import the namespaces into the program.
virtual	Used to create a function that can override a class.
void	Used to declare functions with no specific datatype.
volatile	Used to give a warning to the compiler about the unexpectedly modified variables.
return	Used to return a value from a function.
long	Used to declare a long type of variable which has a bigger space in the memory.
xor	Used as an alternative of ^ OR operator.
this	Used as a pointer to an object.

Table: 2.1 Keywords Used in C++

2.3: Datatypes

A computer can perform functions on different types of data. A set of values and the operation performed on those values are called datatypes. Data is the computer input. which is processed by the computer and it returns the information as an output. In C++, data and the types that can be used are defined at the start of the program.

Different datatypes allowed in C++ are int, float, char, and double.

2.3.1: Integer Datatype

An integer datatype is used to store only numeric digits. It does not support decimal values or fractions. It may include both positive and negative numbers. The programmer must put a (–) minus sign to describe a negative value. By default, it stores positive values.

Different types of integer data are specified according to their size on memory are:

Datatype	Size	Description
Int	2	Store integers from -32,768 to 32,767
Short	2	Store integers from -32,768 to 32,767
unsigned int	2	Store integers from 0 to 65,535
Long	4	Store integers from -2,147,483,648 to 2,147,483,647
unsigned long	4	Store integers from 0 to 4,294,967,295

Table: 2.1 Integer Datatypes

- **Int datatype:**

It is used to store an integer type of data. It takes 2-4 bytes in memory which depends upon the system and compiler being used. It stores integers from -32,768 to 32,767.

- **Short int datatype:**

It is used to store an integer type of data. It takes only 2 bytes in memory which depends upon the system and compiler being used. It stores integers from -32,768 to 32,767.

- **Unsigned datatype:**

It is used to store only positive integer data. It covers 2 bytes in memory. It stores data from 0 to 65,535.

- **Long int datatype:**

Long int used to store large types of integer values. It covers 4 bytes in memory. It stores data from -2,147,483,648 to 2,147,483,647.

- **Unsigned long int datatype:**

Used to store only positive type of integer data. It covers 4 bytes in memory. It stores integers from 0 to 4,294,967,295.

2.3.2: Float Datatype

The float datatype is used to store all real values, including positive and negative integers and decimal point values. It covers 4 bytes in memory. It stores values from +/- 3.4e to +/- 38 (~7 digits).

2.3.3: Double Datatype

Large integer values are stored in double datatype. It covers 8 bytes in memory. It stores data from

+/- 1.7e to +/- 308 (~15 digits).

Datatype	Size	Description
Float	4	Stores from +/- 3.4e to +/- 38 (~7 digits).
Double	8	Stores from +/- 1.7e to +/- 308 (~15 digits).
long double	10	Stores from +/- 1.7e to +/- 308 (~15 digits)

Table: 2.3 Double Datatypes

2.3.4: Char Datatype:

This datatype is used to store all character types of data. It covers 1 byte in memory. A character is used to indicate a letter, number, and other symbols. Character values are commonly input in single quotes, i.e. 'A'.

2.4: Variables

A named memory location or memory cell is called a variable. Variables are used to store input and output data used in the program. The values stored in the variables can be changed during the execution of the program. Variables are stored in the temporary memory of the system and, after the execution of the program, variables stored in the memory are flashed out. Each variable in the program has a unique name that cannot be changed after declaration.

2.4.1: Variable Declaration

The process of describing the variable name and datatype is called a variable declaration. A C++ program can have multiple variables, depending upon the program purpose. Variables must be declared before being used in the program. The programmer can declare a variable anywhere in the program.

The main purpose of the variable declaration is to provide information to the compiler about the data being used in the program. The syntax for a variable declaration is:

data_type variable_name ;

An examples of a variable declaration are:

- int phoneno ;
- char name ;
- float height ;
- double salary ;

In the above examples, int, char, float, and double are the datatypes and phoneno, name, height, and salary are the names.

2.4.2: Rules for Variable Declaration

Some important rules for declaring variables are:

- A variable may include letters, numbers, and underscores (_).

- The variable name must start with a letter or underscore _.

- A variable name must not have blank spaces.

- The variable name may be both in uppercase and lowercase.

- Special characters and reserved words cannot be used in variable names.

- A variable name can be up to 31 characters long in length.

- A name can be used only for one variable.

2.4.3: Variable Initialization

Variable initialization refers to assigning the values to the variable at the time of declaration. The sign used for the initialization is '='. The C++ compiler automatically reserves a memory space when a variable is declared. That memory space will contain some garbage value until a variable is initialized.

The syntax for initializing a variable is:

type_name variable = value ;

Here, type_name is the datatype of the variable, variable is the name of the variable, '=' is the assignment operator and value is the data that is assigned to the variable. Some An examples of variable initialization are:

- Int rollno = 20 ;
- Char section = 'A' ;
- Float average = 90 ;

2.4.4: Variable Scope

The scope is the area or region of the program where a variable can be declared or accessed. A variable cannot be accessed out of its scope so the programmer must keep this in mind when declaring variables.

Variables are divided into two categories, according to their scope.

- **Local Variable:**

A variable that can be only accessed within the function or program body in which it is declared. Its scope is only within that particular function or process. Local variables cannot be accessed outside their scope.

- **Global Variable:**

Global variables are types of variables that can be accessed anywhere in the whole program. These variables exist throughout the execution of the program and can be accessed by any function in a program.

2.5: Constants

Constants in a program indicate a value that cannot be changed during its execution. There are two types of constants in C++ programming - literal constants and symbolic constants.

2.5.1: Literal Constants

A type of constant that is directly written in the program, wherever it is needed, is known as a literal constant. For example:

The following statement indicates the integer literal constant of "50".

Int age = 50 ;

Types of literal constants are:

- **Integer constant:**

Numeric values without any decimal point and fraction are called integer constants. These can include both positive and negative numbers. An examples of integer constant are:

25   96 -35   -41

- **Floating-point constant:**

Constants that can have numeric values with decimal points or fractions are called floating-point constants. A – (minus) sign is placed with the number to display negative values.

- **Character constant:**

All numeric digits, alphabetical, and special symbols written in single quotes are known as character constants. An examples of character constants are:

'K'   '9'   '='   '%'

- **Strings constants:**

String characters refer to a set of characters written inside double quotations. It includes numeric digits, alphabetical, and special symbols. An examples of string characters are:

"XYZ"   "123654"   "55-lord Street, London"

2.5.2: Symbolic Constants

A symbolic constant is a constant that is given to a predefined value that cannot be changed. An example of a symbolic constant is **PI**, used to represent a fixed value of 3.141593. Here, the constant PI can be used anywhere in the program which has its unique fixed value. Symbolic constants have two types:

- define Directive
- const Qualifier

2.6: Expression

The expression refers to a statement that performs one or more operations and provides a value in return. It consists of operands and operators. Operands are the data on which the operations are performed while operators are symbols that perform the operations. An examples of expressions are:

P + Q ;   J * k ;   L / M ;   C + 10 ;

In the first expression "P and Q" are the operands while "+" is an operator sign.

2.7: Operators

Special symbols that are used to perform specific tasks in C++ are called operators. Operators included in C++ are arithmetic operators, assignment operators, relational operators, bitwise operators, logical operators, etc. Categories of operators are as follows:

2.7.1: Unary Operator

Operators that only work on one operand are called unary operators. An examples of unary operators are:

- -- (Decrement operator)
- ++ (increment operator)
- - (pre decrement operator)

27

2.7.2: Binary Operators

Operators that only work with two operands are called binary operators. An examples of binary operators are:

Operator	Operation	Description
+	Addition	Adds two numbers
*	Multiplication	Multiply two numbers
-	Subtraction	Subtracts one number from the second number
/	Division	Divides two numbers
%	Modulus	Provides the remainder of a division operation

Table: 2.4 Binary Operators

To learn how these operators work let's solve an example. Let's suppose we have two numbers stored in variables X and Y. Those numbers are X= 25, Y=5. Apply all arithmetic operators on these numbers.

Operations	Results
A-B	20
A+B	30
A/B	5
A*B	125
A%B	0

Table: 2.5 An example Results

2.7.3: Assignment Statement

This refers to a statement that assigns a value to any variable. An operator known as the assignment operator is used in an assignment statement to assign the values to the variables. The syntax for assignment statement is:

Variable = expression;

An examples of assignment statements are as follows:

- X = 90 ;
- L = M + N ;
- Z = P * Q ;

Lvalue and Rvalue:

In assignment statements, lvalue operand is written on the left side of the assignment operator while rvalue operand is written on the right side of the assignment operator.

2.7.4: Compound Assignment Statement

In the compound assignment statement, one value is assigned to two or more variables at the same time. An assignment operator is used within another assignment operator. An example of an assignment operator is:

- L = M = 50 ;
- K = G = D = 26 ;

2.7.5: Compound Assignment Operators

A type of operator allowed in C++ to combine the assignment operator with an arithmetic operator is called a compound assignment operator. These are used to perform the mathematical operation more effectively. The syntax for a compound assignment operator is:

Variable op = expression ;

In the above syntax "variable" is the variable to the value is assigned, "op" is the operator used as an arithmetic operator, "expression" is any type of constant, variable or expression. An examples of a compound assignment operator are:

- K = K + 50 ;

- K += 50 ;

Both expressions written above perform the same function. They both add a value of 50 in variable K.

2.7.6: Increment Operator

An operator that is used to increment the value of a variable by 1. The symbol used for the increment operator is ++ and it is a unary operator as it deals only a single operand. An increment operator operates only with variables; it does not operate with constants and expressions. There are two types of increment operators that are as follows:

- **Prefix Form:**

The increment operator is written before the operand in prefix form. For example ++M ;

- **Postfix Form:**

The increment operator is written after the operand in the postfix form. For example M++ ;

Both the prefix and postfix operator do the same operation to add the value of a variable by 1. But they both have different effects in program execution.

2.7.7: Decrement Operator

An operator that is used to decrement the value of a variable by 1. The symbol used for the decrement operator is -- and it is a unary operator as it deals only a single operand. The decrement operator operates only with variables it does not operate with constants and expressions. There are two types of decrement operators that are as follows:

- **Prefix Form:**

The decrement operator is written before the operand in prefix form. For example

--M ;

- **Postfix Form:**

The decrement operator is written after the operand in the postfix form. For example M-- ;

In both prefix and postfix operator does the same operation to decrease the value of a variable by 1. But its effects differently in the execution of the program.

2.7.8: Operator Precedence

Operator precedence is an order in which different types of operators are executed in the program. It can also be written as the hierarchy of the operators. In operator precedence, each operator has a unique precedence level that determines which operator will be evaluated first. In C++ the order of operator precedence is as follows:

- () In any expression, first of all, anything inside parentheses will be evaluated.

- * Multiplication and / division symbol will be evaluated right after the parentheses.

- \+ Addition will be done after multiplication or division.

- \- Minus operator will be evaluated at the end of the expression.

Let's solve an example to learn more about the operator precedence.

5 * 10 + 7 * (30 – 10) + 100

1. First of all, the numbers in the parentheses will be evaluated, so the answer after the first evaluation will be 30 – 10 = 20.

   5 * 10 +7 * 20 + 100

2. After that, we will evaluate the multiplication sign. 5 * 10 = 50.

   50 + 7 * 20 + 100

3. Again, we will evaluate the multiplication symbol due to its higher precedence. 7 * 20 = 140.

   50 + 140 + 100

4. After the multiplication, we have to solve the addition operator. 50 + 140 = 190.

   190 + 100

5. Now, we have to evaluate the addition symbol. 190 + 100 = 290.

   290 is the final answer to this expression.

2.7.9: Operator Associativity

An order in which the operators with the same precedence are executed is called operator associativity. When an expression has more than one operator with the same operator precedence, they are executed from left – to – right side or from right – to – left side.

2.7.10: The "sizeof" Operator

An operator used to calculate the size of a variable is called the sizeof operator. It provides the number of bytes occupied in memory by a variable and constant. The syntax for the sizeof operator is:

Sizeof (operand) ;

An examples of the size of the operator are :

- Sizeof (1) ;
- Sizeof (200) ;
- Sizeof (I play football) ;

The output will show the number of bytes occupied in the memory. Like 1 for the character, 2 for the integer, and 15 for the string.

2.8: Type Casting

As it is shown from its name, typecasting refers to changing the type. In C++, it refers to changing the datatype of a variable at the time of execution. There are two major types of typecasting - implicit typecasting, explicit typecasting.

- **Implicit Type Casting:**

A branch of typecasting that is performed automatically by a compiler is called implicit typecasting. An expression that has a different type of data is called mixed-type expression. When an expression has multiple types of variables the solution of the expression will be into the largest datatype available in the expression.

- **Explicit Type Casting:**

A branch of typecasting that is done by the developer or programmer is called explicit typecasting. For this programmer use, an operator called a cast operator which tells the computer to convert the datatype of variable. The syntax for explicit type casting is as follows:

(type) expression ;

In the above syntax, type represents the datatype in which it has to be converted and expression describes the constant, variable, or expression.

2.9: Comments

The lines that are not executed by the compiler are called comments. Comments are written by the programmers to explain the code functions or to troubleshoot it easily when there is an error.

Comments are written to enhance the usability, reliability or troubleshooting of the program. There are multiple types of comments are allowed in the C++ programming language:

- **Single-line comments:**

Comments that are of the single line are called multi-line comments. These comments can be inserted into the program starting with // and ending with //.

- **Multi-line comments:**

Comments that are of more than one line are called multi-line comments. These comments can be inserted into the program starting with /* and ending with */.

Chapter 3

Input and Output

3.1: Standard Input

The word input refers to giving something to the computer. The input is commonly given by the standard keyboards. A program must have some type of input from the user to perform any action. The input given by the keyboard is called standard input. An object that is used to insert input in the C++ program is called **cin**. It stands for Console Input and is used with an insertion operator to give input.

The syntax for using cin is as follows:

cin >> variablename ;

3.2: Standard Output

The word output refers to getting something from a computer system. The output is the result of a program. Most of the time output is displayed on the monitor and is called standard output. An object that is used to display output from the C++ program is called

cout. It stands for Console Output and used with an insertion operator to take output.

The syntax for using cout is as follows:

cout<<variablename;

In C++, we use different streams to perform input and output operations. The word stream refers to the flow of data. These stream objects are declared in the header file, **iostream.h**. This header file must be included in the C++ program to perform input or output actions.

An example Program:

Write a C++ program to enter / insert an integer value in variable and print it on computer screen.

#include < iostream.h >
#include < conio.h >
void main ()
{
clrscr();
int n;
cout<<" Enter any value..! ";
cin>>n;
cout<<" Entered value is = ";
cout<<n;

getch();

}

Output:

Enter any value..!

Entered value is = 10;

// Let's suppose user entered 10.

3.3: Escape Sequence

Special characters that are used to modify the format of output are called escape sequences. Escape sequences are used with backslash "\" and not shown in the output of the program. Escape sequences used in the C++ are:

Description	Escape Sequence
Backspace	\b
Alarm	\a
Form Feed	\f
Carriage Return	\r
Tab	\t
New Line	\n
Single Quote	\'
Double Quote	\"

Table 3.1: Escape Sequence

- **\a:**

It is used to play a beep alarm during the execution of the C++ program. For example:

Write a C++ program to show the use of an Alarm.

#include < iostream.h >

#include < conio.h >

void main ()

{

clrscr();

cout<<"C++ \a Programmer ";

getch();

}

Output: C++ Programmer

After displaying the "**C++**" the system plays a beep and then displays "**Programmer**".

- **\b:**

It is used to insert a backspace in the output of the C++ program. For example:

Write a C++ program to show the use of backspace.

#include < iostream.h >

```
#include < conio.h >
void main ()
{
clrscr();
cout<<" C++ \b Programmer ";
getch();
}
```

Output: C+Programmer

First of all "**C++**" is displayed then "\b" deletes the "+". After that "**Programmer**" will be printed.

- \f:

It is used to insert a blank paper in the output of the C++ program. For example:

Write a C++ program to show the use of Form Feed.

```
#include < iostream.h >
#include < conio.h >
void main ()
{
clrscr();
cout<<" C++ \f Programmer ";
```

getch();

}

Output: C++

Programmer

After displaying "**C++**" there will be a blank page then display "**Programmer**".

- \n:

It is used to add a new line in the output of the C++ program. For example:

Write a C++ program to show the use of the New Line.

#include < iostream.h >

#include < conio.h >

void main ()

{

clrscr();

cout<<" C++ \n Programmer ";

getch();

}

Output: C++

    Programmer

After displaying "**C++**" there will be a blank line then display "**Programmer**".

- \r:

It is used to shift the cursor at the start of the line. For example:

Write a C++ program to show the use of Carriage Return.

#include < iostream.h >

#include < conio.h >

void main ()

{

clrscr();

cout<<" C++ \r Programmer ";

getch();

}

Output: Programmer

After displaying "**C++**" control moves to the start of the line and display "**Programmer**" which overwrites C++.

- \t:

It is used to add a TAB space in the output of the C++ program. For example:

Write a C++ program to show the use of TAB.

#include < iostream.h >
#include < conio.h >
void main ()
{
clrscr();
cout<<" C++ \t Programmer ";
getch();
}

Output: C++   Programmer

After displaying "**C++**" there will be a TAB space and then display "**Programmer**".

- \':

It is used to insert a single quote in the output of the C++ program. For example:

Write a C++ program to show the use of Single Quote.

#include < iostream.h >
#include < conio.h >
void main ()
{

clrscr();

cout<<" \' C++ Programmer \' ";

getch();

}

Output: 'C++Programmer'

- \":

It is used to insert a double quote in the output of the C++ program. For example:

Write a C++ program to show the use of Carriage Return.

#include < iostream.h >

#include < conio.h >

void main ()

{

clrscr();

cout<<" \" C++ Programmer \' ";

getch();

}

Output: "C++ Programmer"

3.4: C++ Manipulators

Reserved words that are used to format the output in different styles are called manipulators. These are the most effective way to manage the output formatting.

Manipulators commonly used in C++ are:

- **endl;**

It stands for **the end of the line** and used to move the cursor to the next line in the output of the program. endl is the replica of \n (the escape character). An example:

cout<<" C++ "<<endl<<" Programmer ";

Output:

    C++

Programmer

- **set:**

It stands for **set width** and is used to print the value of an expression in specific columns. The syntax for the set width is:

Set(n)

Here n is the number of columns from which the value has to be displayed.

- **setprecision;**

It stands for **set precision** and used to set the number of digits to be displayed after the decimal point. The syntax for setprecision is:

setprecision(n);

here n is the number of displayed after the decimal point.

- **Setfill;**

By using setfill loading or trailing blanks are replaced by the specified characters in the program output. An example:

cout<<"C++"<<endl<<setfill<<"Programmer";

Output:
C++PROGRAMMER:

- **showpoint;**

It stands for "**show point**", and used to the decimal part of a number even if it is zero in the output of the program. The syntax for showpoint is:

cout << showpoint;

- **fixed;**

It is used to manage the output of floating-point numbers in a fixed decimal format. The syntax for fixed is:

cout<<fixed;

Practice Exercise 1

1. Write a program in C++ that inputs a number from the user and displays the ASCII code of that number.

2. Write a program in C++ that inputs the roll no, name, class, section, and height from a student and display all the values on the screen with a one-line break.

3. Write a C++ program that inputs 2 numbers and swap that without creating the third variable.

4. Write a Program in C++ that takes height and the base from the user. Use that inputs to calculate the area of a triangle.

5. Write a program that inputs time in hours from the user and convert it into minutes and seconds and displays the answer in new lines.

6. Write a program in C++ that takes a number as an input. Find the reverse of that number by implementing your logic.

7. Write a C++ program that inputs age from a user in days and convert it into the month, and years.

8. Write a C++ program that displays the following results on the screen using cout statement.

    | 9 | 8 | 7 | 6 | 5 |
    | 4 | 3 | 2 | 1 | 0 |

9. Write a Program in C++ that will take 5 numbers as an input and display their sum, product, and average.

10. Write a program that will display the following out by using cout statement and escape sequences.

```
*
**
***
****
*****
******
*******
********
*********
```

Solution Practice Exercise 1

1. Write a program in C++ that inputs a number from the user and displays the ASCII code of that number.

```
#include < iostream.h >
#include < conio.h >
void main ()
{
clrscr();
char input;
int n = input;
cout<<" Enter any Character = ";
cin>>input;
cout<<" ASCII Code of the character is = "<<n<<endl;
getch();
}
```

Output:

Enter any Character = a

ASCII code of the character is = 97

2. Write a program in C++ that inputs the roll no, name, class, section, and height from a student and displays all the values on the screen with a one-line break.

```cpp
#include < iostream.h >
#include < conio.h >
void main ()
{
clrscr();
int rollno;
char name[10], class[10];
float height;
cout<<" Enter Roll no = ";
cin>>rollno;
cout<<" Enter Name = ";
cin>>name;
cout<<" Enter Class = ";
cin>>class;
cout<<" Enter Height = ";
cin>>height;
cout<<" Your Roll no is = " <<rollno<<endl;
cout<<" Your Name is = " <<name<<endl;
cout<<" Your Class is = " <<class<<endl;
```

cout<<" Your Height is = " <<height<<endl;

getch();

}

Output:

Your Roll No is = 90

Your Name is = Michael

Your Class is = A Level

Your Height is = 5.9"

3. Write a C++ program that inputs 2 numbers and swap that without creating the third variable.

#include < iostream.h >

#include < conio.h >

void main ()

{

clrscr();

int a, b;

cout<<" Enter two numbers = ";

cin>>a;

cin>>b;

cout<<" Numbers Before swapping are = " <<a<<endl;

```
cout<<b<<endl;
a = a = b;
b = a – b;
a = a – b;
cout<<" Numbers After Swapping are = "<<endl;
cout<<a<<endl;
cout<<b<<endl;
getch();
}
```

Output:

Numbers Before Swapping = 9

                                6

Numbers After Swapping = 6

                                9

4. Write a Program in C++ that takes height and the base from the user. Use that inputs to calculate the area of a triangle.

```
#include < iostream.h >
#include < conio.h >
void main ()
{
```

```
clrscr();
int height;
int base;
int area;
cout<<" Enter height = ";
cin>>height;
cout<<" Enter base = ";
cin>>base;
area = ½*base*height;
cout<<" Area of triangle is = "<<area<<endl;
getch();
}
```

Output:

Enter base = 20

Height = 10

Area of triangle is = 100=

5. Write a program that inputs time in hours from the user and convert it into minutes and seconds and displays the answer in new lines.

```
#include < iostream.h >
#include < conio.h >
```

```
void main ()
{
clrscr();
int hours;
cout<<" Enter time in hours = ";
cin>>hours;
cout<<" Time in minutes is = " <<hours * 60<<endl;
cout<<" Time in seconds is = " <<hours * 60 * 60<>endl;
getch();
}
```

Output:

Enter time in hours = 6

Time in Minutes = 360

Time in seconds = 21,600

6. Write a program in C++ that takes a number as an input. Find the reverse of that number by implementing your logic.

```
#include < iostream.h >
#include < conio.h >
void main ()
```

{

clrscr();

long int a, b, c, d, e, f;

cout<<" Enter five digits = ";

cin>>a;

b = a / 10000;

a = a % 10000;

c = a / 10000;

a = a % 10000;

d = a / 10000;

a = a % 10000;

e = a / 10000;

a = a % 10000;

f = a / 10000;

a = a % 10000;

cout<<" Reverse number is = " <<a <<b <<c <<d <<e <<f <<endl;

getch();

}

Output:

Enter five digits = 9 4 6 3 5

Digits in reverse order are = 5 3 6 4 9

7. Write a C++ program that inputs age from the user in days and convert it into the month, and years.

```
#include <iostream.h>
#include <conio.h>
void main ()
{
clrscr();
int day;
cout<<"Enter days = ";
cin>>day;
cout<<" In months = "<<day / 30<<endl;
cout<<" In months = "<<day / 365<<endl;
getch();
}
```

Output:

Enter days = 730

In months = 24

In years = 2

8. Write a C++ program that displays the following results on the screen using cout statement.

    9   8   7   6   5

4   3   2   1   0

```
#include < iostream.h >
#include < conio.h >
void main ()
{
clrscr();
cout<<" 9 \t 8 \t 7 \t 6 \t 5 " <<endl;
cout<<" 4 \t 3 \t 2 \t 1 \t 0 " <<endl;
getch();
}
```

Output:

9   8   7   6   5
4   3   2   1   0

9. Write a Program in C++ that will take 5 numbers as an input and display their sum, product, and average.

```
#include < iostream.h >
#include < conio.h >
void main ()
{
clrscr();
int a, b, c, d, e;
```

```
        cout<<"Enter five numbers = ";
        cin>> a>> b>> c>> d>> e>>endl;
        cout<<" Sum of digits   ="<<a + b + c + d +
e<<endl;
        cout<<" product of digits   ="<<a * b * c * d *
e<<endl;
        cout<<" average of digits  ="<<(a + b + c + d + e)
/ 5<<endl;
        getch();
        }
```

Output:

Enter five numbers = 2 4 6 8 10

Sum of digits = 30

Product of digits = 3840

Average of digits = 6

10. Write a program that will display the following out by using cout statement and escape sequences.

*
**
***
****
*****
******
****
****
****

#include < iostream.h >

#include < conio.h >

void main ()

{

cout<<" * " <<endl;

cout<<" ** " <<endl;

cout<<" *** " <<endl;

cout<<" **** " <<endl;

cout<<" ***** " <<endl;

```
cout<<" ****** " <<endl;

cout<<" ******* " <<endl;
cout<<" ******** " <<endl;

cout<<" ********* " <<endl;

cout<<" ********** " <<endl;
getch();
}
```

Output:

```
*
**
***
****
*****
******
*******
********
*********
**********
```

Chapter 4

Structures

4.1: Control Structure

A statement or set of statements that are used to control the flow of execution of a C++ program is known as a Control Structure. The flow of execution in a program can be managed by three types of control structures. These control structures are used in the implementation of the program's real logic.

4.1.1: Types of Control Structures

There are 4 types of program structures discussed below: (These are discussed in detail in the first chapter)

- **Sequence**
- **Selection**
- **Repetition**
- **Function Call**

4.2: Relational Operators

Operators that are used to determine the conditions in a program are called Relational Operator. The relational operator always compares two values and produces the results as **"TRUE"** or **"FALSE"**. Relational operators are also known as conditional operators. The relational operator checks a condition and generates the results according to the condition test. Relational operators used in C++ programming language are:

Operators	Description
>	It is used to check the greater number and returns "TRUE" if the condition remains true.
<	It is used to check the lesser value and returns "TRUE" if the condition remains true.
==	Equal to operator used to compare the left-hand side with the right-hand side. It returns "TRUE" is both sides are same or return "FALSE" if both sides are different.
>=	Greater than or equal to the operator compares two values and returns "TRUE" if the left-hand side is greater or equal to the right-hand side. Or returns "FALSE" if the left-hand side is not greater or equal to the right.
<=	Less than or equal to the operator compares two values and returns "TRUE" if the left-hand side is lesser or equal to the right-hand side. Or

	returns "FALSE" if the left-hand side is not lesser or equal to the right.
!=	Not equal to the operator is used to check the non-equality. It returns "TRUE" if both values are not equal to each other. Or returns "FALSE" if both sides are equal to each other.

Table 4.1: Relational Operators

4.2.1: Relational Expression

A statement that contains different relational operators to contrast values is called a relational expression. The result produced by the relational expression is only "TRUE" and "FALSE". Here are some An examples of relational expressions.

Relational Expression	Result
200 < 98	FALSE
29 > 6	TRUE
5! = 14	TRUE
9 >=9	TRUE
16 = = 19	FALSE
4 <= 60	TRUE
48 >= 20	TRUE

Table 4.2: Relational Expression

4.3: 'if' Statement

It is a keyword in the C++ programming language. It works as a decision-making statement. An if statement is the simplest selection structure and works by executing or skipping a statement or statements by evaluating a condition. If the condition remains TRUE, the statements or set of statements are executed after the condition. If the condition remains FALSE, the statements after the if the condition will be skipped.

The syntax for if the statement is as follows:

if (condition)

statement;

It is used for a single statement. When there are multiple statements a compound if statement is used.

The syntax for compound if statements is:

if (condition)

{

statement a;

statement b;

.

.

.

statement n;

}

4.3.1: Limitations for 'if' Statement

As we know, the if statement executes a statement or set of statements by evaluating a condition. It executes if the condition is true and does nothing when the condition is false. When a user wants to execute some statements when the condition remains false then a simple 'if' is not applicable.

An example: Write a program that inputs two numbers and display TRUE if the numbers are equals by evaluating the if statement.

```
#include < iostream.h >
#include < conio.h >
void main ()
{
clrscr();
int n, m;
cout<<" Enter any number = ";
cin>>n;
cout<<" Enter any number = ";
cin>>m;
if (n>m)
{
cout<<" TRUE " <<endl;
}
getch();
}
```

Output:

Enter any number = 45

Enter any number = 90

TRUE

4.4: 'if-else' Statement

The if-else statement is the advanced form of the if statement. The if-else statement executes one block of code if the given condition is true, and executes another block or code when the condition remains false. An if-else statement must execute one block whether the statement remains true or false.

If-else statement works on two rules:

- It cannot execute both blocks of code at the same time.
- It cannot skip both blocks of code at the same time.

The syntax for if-else statement is:

If (condition)

Statement;

else

Statement;

The syntax for compound statements:

If (condition)

{

Statement 1;

Statement 2;

.

.

.

.

Statement n;

}

else

{

Statement 1;

Statement 2;

.

.

.

.

Statement n;

}

An example: Write a C++ program that will input 2 numbers and show the highest number using an if-else statement.

```cpp
#include < iostream.h >
#include < conio.h >
void main ()
{
clrscr();
int a, b;
cout<<" Enter any number = ";
cin>>a;
cout<<" Enter any number = ";
cin>>b;
if (a > b )
{
cout<<" Greater number is" <<a <<endl;
}
Else
{
cout<<" Greater number is" <<b <<endl;
}
getch();
}
```

Output:

Enter any number = 45

Enter any number = 90

The greater number is B = 90

4.5: Multiple 'if-else-if' Statement

An if-else-if statement executes a single block of statements from a multiple blocks of the statements. It is used when there are multiple blocks are available and we have to execute only one block by evaluating a condition.

The syntax for the multiple if-else statement is:

If (condition)

{

Block a;

}

Else-if

{

Block b

}

Else-if

{

Block c;

}

Else

{

Block d;

}

Working of the multiple if-else statements:

In the if-else-if statement, control comes to the first condition and checks the condition. If the condition is true, the block of code right after the condition will be executed. If the condition is false, control moves to the next condition. The process repeats until the condition is true. If the condition is never true, the block after the last else will be executed.

An example: Write a program that takes three numbers and shows the lowest number.

#include < iostream.h >

#include < conio.h >

void main ()

{

clrscr();

int a, b, c;

cout<<" Enter any number = ";

cin>>a;

cout<<" Enter any number = ";

```
cin>>b;
cout<<" Enter any number = ";
cin>>c;
if (a < b && a < c)
{
cout<<" Smallest number is" <<a <<endl;
}
Else-if
if (b < c && b < a)
{
cout<<" Smallest number is" <<b <<endl;
}
else
{
cout<<" Smallest number is" <<c <<endl;
}
getch();
}
```

Output:

Enter any number = 45

Enter any number = 90

Enter any Number = 11

Smallest number is = 11

4.6: Nested 'if' Statement

An if statement which has another if statement in it is known as a Nested if statement. It is used when the user has to validate a condition within another condition. First of all, control enter into the first loop and check the condition; if the condition remains true, control enters into the inner condition. If the inner condition remains true, the block of statements after the inner condition will be executed. Otherwise, control exits from the block.

The syntax for nested if the statement is:

If (condition)
   If (condition)
   {
   Statement (n);
   }
   else
   {
   Statement (n);
   }
Else
{
Statement (n);
}

An example: Write a C++ program that inputs three numbers and displays the second highest among them.

```
#include < iostream.h >
#include < conio.h >
void main ()
{
clrscr();
int x, y, z;
cout<<" Enter any number = ";
cin>>x;
cout<<" Enter any number = ";
cin>>y;
cout<<" Enter any number = ";
cin>>z;
if (x > y)
    if (x > z)
    {
    cout<<" second Biggest number is" <<x <<endl;
    }
    else
    {
    cout<<"second  Biggest number is" <<z <<endl;
    }
```

Else

if (y < z)

{

cout<<" second Biggest number is" <<y <<endl;

}

else

{

cout<<" second Biggest number is" <<z <<endl;

}

getch();

}

4.7: Compound Condition

When there are more than one conditions to check, programmers use a compound condition to perform their tasks. It is used to evaluate the statement or block of statements by checking conditions. Different types of compound operators are as follows:

4.7.1: Logical Operators

Operators that are used to validate compound conditions called logical operators. There are three types of logical operators used in the C++ programming language:

- **AND Operator (&&):**

AND operator is used to check two conditions. It returns "TRUE" if both of the conditions are true, and it returns "FALSE" when both of the statements are wrong. (&&) is the specific symbol used to represent AND operator?

Condition 1	Operator	Condition 2	Result
True	&&	True	True
True	&&	False	False
False	&&	True	False
False	&&	False	False

Table 4.3: Logical AND Operator

- **NOT Operator (!);**

NOT operator is used to evaluate two conditions. It returns "TRUE" if both of the conditions are true, and it returns "FALSE" when both of the statements are wrong. (!) is the specific symbol used to represent the NOT operator?

Operator	Condition	Result
!	True	False
!	False	True

Table 4.5: Logical NOT Operator

- **OR Operator (||):**

OR operator is used to validating compound conditions. It returns "TRUE" if either one of the conditions remains true, and it returns "FALSE" when any of the statements are wrong. (||) is the specific symbol used to represent AND operator?

Condition 1	Operator	Condition 2	Result
True	||	True	True
True	||	False	True
False	||	True	True
False	||	False	False

Table 4.4: Logical OR Operator

4.8: Switch Statement

The switch statement is known as a conditional structure. It is the best replacement for the nested if-else statement. It is used when there are multiple choices available and we only have to select one of them. The switch statement operates by evaluating an expression.

The syntax for switch statement is as follows:

Switch (expression)

{

Case 1:

Statement (s);

Break;

Case 2:

Statement (s);

Break;

.

.

.

Case n:

Statement (s);

Break;

Default:

Statement (n);

}

Working of a switch statement:

First of all, control enters the first expression and evaluates it. If the answer matches the case value, the statements right after that expression will be executed. The process does the same for all of the cases. If the expression does not match with any case, the default case will be executed and the block of statements after the default will be executed.

An example of a switch statement is:

Write a program that will input a number from the user and display the day of the week corresponding to that number.

```
#include < iostream.h >
#include < conio.h >
void main ()
{
clrscr();
int a;
cout<<" Enter any number between 1 – 7 = ";
cin>>a;
switch(a)
{
Case 1:
Cout<<" Monday ";
Break;
Case 2:
Cout<<" Tuesday ";
Break;
Case 3:
Cout<<" Wednesday ";
Break;
Case 4:
Cout<<" Thursday ";
```

Break;

Case 5:

Cout<<" Friday ";

Break;

Case 6:

Cout<<" Saturday ";

Break;

Case 7:

Cout<<" Sunday";

Break;

Default:

Cout<<" Invalid Number ";

getch();

}

Output:

Enter any number between 1 – 7 = 5

Friday

4.9: Conditional Operator

It is a decision-making operator that is used as an alternative to a simple if-else statement. It is also known as the ternary operator. The syntax for the conditional operator is:

(condition) ? true-case statement : false-case statement;

Here, the conditions are the logical or relational expressions; it evaluates the condition and returns TRUE or FALSE. If the expression becomes true, the true-case is executed. If the expression becomes false, the false-case is executed.

4.10: 'goto' Statement

This statement is used to jump to a particular area of the C++ program by using the label. The label is the name that is assigned to the particular statement of the program where you want to shift the control.

The syntax for the goto statement is:

goto Label;

How the goto statement works:
When control reaches to goto statement it reads the label which is usually the address of the states where you want to move the control of the program.

Practice Exercise 2

1. Write a C++ program that inputs two numbers from the user and display whether all the numbers are equal or not using the if-else-if statement.

2. Write a program that enters three numbers and display the biggest number by using logical operators.

3. Write a program in C++ that inputs a character from the user and displays it is a vowel or not.

4. Write a C++ program that inputs a number and displays whether it is an even number or an odd number by using logical operators.

5. Write a program that enters a number and displays whether it is divisible by 5 or not.

6. Write a program that prints "Hello World" on the screen for times by using the goto statement.

7. Write a program that will input a case from the user and convert the temperature from degree to Fahrenheit or Celsius and from Fahrenheit to degree and Celsius according to the user's input. Use switch statement logic to implement this logic

8. Write a program that will input a number from the user and shows whether it is a leap year or not.

9. Write a program that enters salary and rank. It adds a 40% bonus if the rank is greater than the 17. It adds 30% if the rank is greater than 14. It adds 15% if the rank is greater than 11. Displays the final salary of the employee.

10. Write a program that will print welcome messages on screen if the user enters a number greater than 6 and displays a sign off message if the user enters a number below than 6. By using a conditional operator.

Chapter 5

Looping Structures

5.1: Loops

A specific type of control structure that repeats a statement or block of statements is called a looping structure. The looping structure is also known as a repetitive or iterative structure. Sequential structures execute all the statements once, while conditional structures execute or skip all the statements by validating a condition. But sometimes we need a statement or block of statements to be executed repeatedly. For this purpose, we use loops in programming languages. Two main categories of loops used in C++ are counter-control loops and control loops.

5.1.1: Counter-Controlled Loops

A type of loop that depends on the value of a variable called counter variable. The counter variable is the most essential part and the value in this variable is incremented or decremented on each iteration. Counter-controlled loop exits when the value stored in the counter variable reaches a specific value. In the counter-controlled loop, the number of iterations is predefined.

The execution of the counter-controlled loop relies on:

- The initial value of the counter variable.
- Loop exiting condition
- Increment and decrement operator

5.1.2: Sentinel-Controlled Loops

A type of loop that depends on a special value called sentinel value is called a sentinel-controlled loop. The loop exits the control when the sentinel value remains false. Sentinel-controlled loops are also called conditional loops. In sentinel-controlled loops, the number of iterations is not defined or known. It runs until a sentinel value is encountered. It is usually used in while or do-while loop.

5.2: 'while' Loop

The simplest loop in the C++ programming language is known as while loop. A while loop executes statements until the given condition remains **TRUE** and is used when the number of iterations is not known before execution. It is also called a pretest loop. The syntax for the while loop is:

While (condition)

Statement;

The syntax for while loop for compound statements is:

While (condition)

{

statement a;

statement b;

.

.

.

Statement;

}

Working on while loop:

When control of the program reaches to the while loop. It evaluates the condition. If the condition remains it executes the statements and move to the condition and again evaluate it. Hence the execution of loop runs until the condition remains false.

An example: Write a program that displays a "Welcome to the school" greeting message on the screen five times using a while loop.

#include <iostream.h>

#include <conio.h>

void main ()

{

int a = 1;

clrscr ();

while (a <= 5)

```
{
cout<<" Welcome to the school "<<endl;
a++;
}
getch();
}
```

Output:

Welcome to the school

Welcome to the school

Welcome to the school

Welcome to the school

Welcome to the school

An example: Write a program that displays counting from 90 – 100 in descending order on the screen using a while loop.

```
#include <iostream.h>
#include <conio.h>
void main ()
{
int x = 1, y = 100;
clrscr ();
```

```
while (x <= 10)
{
cout<<" y "<<endl;
y--;
x++;
}
getch();
}
```

Output:

100

99

98

97

96

95

94

93

92

91

90

5.3: 'do-while' Loop

An iterative control structure in the C++ programming language is known as a do-while loop. The do-while loop is used to execute the body of the program at least once. Because the condition in the do-while loop comes after the program statements, it is also called a post-test loop. The syntax for the do-while loop is:

do
{
statement a;
statement b;
.
.
.
statement n;
}
While (condition);

Working of the do-while loop:

When control reaches the loop the program body, the program is executed for the first time. After the execution of the program, the condition of the statement is evaluated. It executes the statements again and again until the condition remains true.

An example: Write a program that displays counting from 1 – 20 in a one-line order on the screen using a do-while loop.

```
#include <iostream.h>
#include <conio.h>
void main ()
{
clrscr ();
int a = 1;
do
{
cout<<" a \t " ;
a = a + 1;
}
while (a <= 20);
getch();
}
```

Output:
1 2 3 4 5 6 7 8 9 10 11 12 13 14 15 16 17 18 19 20

5.4: 'for' Loop

A loop that is used to execute statements for a specific number of times is called a for loop. A for loop is also known as a counter-controlled loop and it is the most frequently used loop in the C++ programming language. Execution of a for loop is based on a special counter variable. The syntax for the for loop is:

for (initialization; condition; increment/decrement operator)

{

statement a;

statement b;

.

.

.

statement n;

}

Working of for loop:

How a for loop works depends on the initialization, increment or decrement, and condition. When control enters the loop, it initializes the value of a counter variable. Then the condition is checked, and the increment or decrement operator is processed, and the statements are executed until the condition remains true.

An example: Write a program that displays the sum of all numbers from 1 – 10 on the screen using for loop.

```
#include <iostream.h>
#include<conio.h>
void main ()
{
clrscr ();
long int num = 0;
int a;
for (a = 1; a <= 10; a++)
{
num = num + 1;
cout<<" Result is = "<<num<<endl ;
}
getch();
}
```

5.4.1: 'continue' Statement

The continue statement is a specific type of statement which has a predefined task. It is used to move the control to the start of the program body. When the continue statement is executed in the program body, the remaining statements are skipped, and control moves to the start of the body.

An example: Write a program that displays a message on screen five times by using a continue statement.

```cpp
#include <iostream.h>
#include <conio.h>
void main ()
{
clrscr ();
int a;
for (a = 1; a <= 5; a++)
{
cout<<" I love programming "<<endl;
continue;
cout<<" knowledge is light "<<endl;
}
getch();
}
```

Output:

I love programming

I love programming

I love programming

I love programming

I love programming

Working of continue statement:

When control enters the loop body it checks the condition and executes the statements after the condition. When control moves to continue the statement, it skips the rest of the program statements and moves to the start of the loop. Loop will be executed until the condition becomes false.

5.4.2: 'break Statement

The break statement is used to terminate the loop execution. When a break statement occurs in a program, control moves out from the loop body and the remaining iterations of the loop are not executed.

An example: Write a program that breaks the loop execution at the third iteration and displays a message at each iteration.

```
#include <iostream.h>
#include <conio.h>
void main ()
{
clrscr ();
int a;
for (a = 1; a <= 5; a++)
{
cout<<" Hello World "<<endl;
if (a = 3)
break;
```

}

cout<<" Execution Terminated "<<endl;

}

getch();

}

Output:

Hello World

Hello World

Hello World

Execution Terminated

Working of break statement:

When the loop starts, it will be executed three times and, every time, the value of increment operator will be raised by one. And when the value of the counter variable reaches three, control exits the loop body and execute the statements outside of the loop.

5.5: Nested Loops

A loop within another loop is known as a nested loop. In nested loops, the inner block of statements is executed completely at each iteration of the outer loop. Many nested loops increase the complexity of the program. We can use any type of loop as an inner or outer loop in nested loops.

The syntax for nested loops are:

for (initialization: condition: increment/decrement)

{

    for (initialization: condition: increment/decrement)

    {

    Statement (n);

    }

}

An example: Write a program that the following output using nested lops.

*****

****

***

**

*

#include <iostream.h>

#include <conio.h>

void main ()

{

clrscr ();

int x, y;

for (x = 1; x <= 5; x++)

```
{
    x = y;
    while (y<=7)
    {
        Cout<< "*";
        y++;
    }
cout<<" \n";
}
getch();
}
```

Output:

*****

****

***

**

*

Working of nested loops:

When control reaches the first loop it will check the condition and enters the loop if the condition is true. It will again check the condition of the inner loop and executes it until the condition remains true. After executing the inner loop control exits and checks the outer loop condition. The inner loop will be executed completely on each iteration of the outer loop.

Practice Exercise 3

1. Write a C++ program that inputs 5 numbers from user prints numbers with their cubes by using a while loop.

2. Write a program that enters a number and displays its table in reverse order by using a while loop.

3. Write a program in C++ that inputs a number from the user and displays the product of its digits by using a while loop.

4. Write a C++ program that inputs a number and displays its factorial using while loop.

5. Write a program that enters a number and displays whether it is divisible by 5 or not.

6. Write a program that prints the following output by using a while loop.

   Number   Product
   ----
   1   1

2	2
3	6
4	24
5	120

----

7. Write a program that displays all alphabets in reverse order using for loop.

8. Write a program that will input n numbers from the user and display the biggest, smallest, and average of that numbers.

9. Write a program that adds the sequence of integer numbers considering that the first integer specifies the number of values remaining to be input. The program must read the value at every input. A typical sequence of input maybe 10 100 200 150 300 500. The first number shows that the subsequent 10 coming values have to be added.

10. Write a program that will input a number from the user and displays all the odd numbers less than that number by using a loop.

11. Write a C++ program to display the following output.

```
* * * * * * * * *
*               *
*               *
*               *
```

```
        *              *
        *              *
        *              *
        *              *
        *              *
        * * * * * * * * *
```

12. Write a C++ program that will prints the following output on the screen.

    ```
    5  4  3  2  1
    5  4  3  2
    5  4  3
    5  4
    5
    ```

13. Write a program n C++ that will prints the following output on the screen using loops.

    ```
              1
             222
            33333
           4444444
          555555555
         66666666666
        7777777777777
    ```

888888888888888

999999999999999999

14. Write a C++ program that will prints the following output on the screen.

    0

    2 4

    6 8 10

    12 14 16

    18 20 22 24

    26 28 30 32 34

    36 38 40 42 44 46

    48 50 52 54 56 58 60

15. Write a C++ program that will print the following output on the screen.

$
$$
$$$
$$$$
$$$$$
$$$$
$$$
$$
$

16. Write a C++ program that will prints the following output on the screen.

    6 5 4 3 2 1 0 1 2 3 4 5 6

    6 5 4 3 2 1   1 2 3 4 5 6

    6 5 4 3 2   2 3 4 5 6

    6 5 4 3   3 4 5 6

    6 5 4   4 5 6

    6 5   5 6

    6   6

17. Write a C++ program that will print all the combinations of 1, 2, 3 by using loops.

18. Write a C++ program that displays total sum the following series by using do-while loop.

    $1 + \frac{1}{2} + \frac{1}{4} + 1/6 + \ldots + 1/100$.

19. Write a C++ program that will print the following output on the screen.

    1

    2 4

    3 6 9

    2 4

    1

20. Write a C++ program that will prints the following output on the screen.

    1 = 1
    1 + 2 = 3
    1 + 2 + 3 = 6
    1 + 2 + 3 + 4 = 10
    1 + 2 + 3 + 4 + 5 = 15

Chapter 6

Arrays

6.1: Introduction to Arrays

A simple group of consecutive memory locations with the same specific name and datatype is called an Array. A simple variable is a single block of memory location with a specific name and a type. On the other hand, an array is a collective memory location with a specified name. It is used to store a large amount of collective data. These memory locations are known as elements of the array.

Data stored in an array is accessed regarding its location in the array. Each position in an array is known as an index. The first index of the array is o and the last index is known as n-1. Arrays are used to store a large amount of collective data. For example, when a user wants to store 100 data values in the memory it will be stored in an array instead of creating 100 values. Arrays are used to access the data more quickly and easily.

6.1.1: Declaration of One-Dimensional Array

One type of array is a one-dimensional array. It is also known as a single-dimensional array or linear list. The process of assigning the array name, length and datatype is called an array declaration.

The syntax for declaring a one-dimensional array is:

Data_type identifier [Length];

An example:

int marks [10];

The above An example declares an integer array marks of 10 elements. It allocates 10 consecutive locations in the memory.

Indexes of array	0	1	2	3	4	5	6	7	8	9
Values of array	29	56	24	36	87	96	71	47	40	30

6.1.2: Array Initialization

The process of assigning values to an array at the time of declaration is called array initialization. In this phase, the array is assigned the list of initial values. All values are separated by a comma sign ',' and are enclosed within the curly-braces.

The syntax for array initialization is:

int marks [10] = (29, 56, 24, 36, 87, 96, 71, 47, 40, 30);

Indexes of array	0	1	2	3	4	5	6	7	8	9
Values of array	29	56	24	36	87	96	71	47	40	30

6.1.3: Accessing Individual Elements of Array

In one-dimensional array each individual element is accessed by following steps:

- Name of an array
- Index of element

The syntax for accessing an individual element of an array is:

Array_Name [index];

An example:

int marks [10];

marks [0] = 29;

marks [0] = 56;

marks [0] = 24;

marks [0] = 36;

marks [0] = 87;

marks [0] = 96;

marks [0] = 71;

marks [0] = 47;

marks [0] = 40;

marks [0] = 30;

In the above An example, the array is declared as marks of 10 indexes. Elements in the array are accessed by using the array name with the specific index number.

6.1.4: *Accessing the Array Elements using Loops*

Accessing an array element by using loops is an efficient and faster way of accessing the elements. Let's have a look at how the array is accessed using loops.

```
int marks [10];
for (int x = 0; x<10; x++)
{
marks [x] = x;
cout<<" x "<<endl;
}
```

In the above An example, elements in the array are accessed using a for loop. We have initiated the counter variable in the loop with "0" to access the array from the first index. This code will display all the index values on the screen.

6.1.5: *Input and Output Values of an Array*

The process of inputting and getting output from an array is similar to the variables. Arrays are input using the keyword "cin" and for getting output, the keyword "cout" is used.

An examples to know how we input or access an array without using loops.

Write a program that will input five values from a user and display the output without using loops.

```
#include <iostream.h>
#include <conio.h>
void main ()
{
clrscr ();
int abc [5];
cout<<" Enter a number "<<endl;
cin>>abc [0];
cin>>abc [1];
cin>>abc [2];
cin>>abc [3];
cin>>abc [4];
cout<<" Values entered by user are: "<<endl;
cout<< abc [0] <<endl;
cout<< abc [1] <<endl;
cout<< abc [2] <<endl;
cout<< abc [3] <<endl;
cout<< abc [4] <<endl;
}
```

getch();

}

Output:

Enter a number: 2

Enter a number: 7

Enter a number: 6

Enter a number: 10

Enter a number: 21

Values entered by the user are:

2

7

6

10

An example: Write a program that will input five values from user and display the output using loops.

#include <iostream.h>

#include <conio.h>

void main ()

```
{
clrscr ();
int abc [5];
for (int x = 0; x <= 5; x++)
{
cout<<" Enter a number "<<endl;

   cin>>abc [x];
}
cout<<" Values entered by user are: "<<endl;
for (int x = 0; x <= 5; x++)
{
cout<< abc [x] <<endl;
}
getch();
}
```

Output:

Enter a number: 2

Enter a number: 7

Enter a number: 6

Enter a number: 10

Enter a number: 21

Values entered by the user are:

2

7

6

10

21

6.2: Searching in Arrays

A process of finding values from an array is called searching. Searching is much important when there is a long array and we have to search for data from it. Types of searches are sequential search and binary search.

6.2.1: Sequential Search

The simplest way of searching values from an array is linear or sequential search. A sequential search is done in the following steps.

- Visit the first index and compare the values in the indexes.

- If the value compared matches with the required value, the search is completed.

- If the values do not match with the desired value it moves to the next index.

An example: write a program that inputs an array from a user and search for a value from the array by using a sequential search.

```
#include <iostream.h>
#include <conio.h>
void main ()
{
clrscr ();
int abc [5] = 1, 2, 3, 4, 5;
int x, y, loc = -1;
cout<<" Enter a number to find "<<endl;
cin>> y;
for (int x = 0; x < 5; x++)
{
if (abc [x] == x)
loc = x;
if (loc == -1)
cout<<" number not found "<<endl;
 else
cout<<" number found at index "<<loc<<endl;
}
getch();
}
```

Output:

Enter a number to find: 6

Number not found

How Does It work?

First of all, an array of five integers is declared or initialized. Then the user will input the number that has to be searched from the array. Using the loop, the program will compare the desired value with each index of an array. If value matches with the index element, it terminates the search and displays the index from which the value is matched.

6.2.2: Binary Search

A quicker method of searching from an array is called a binary search. It is a faster method of search but, it can be implemented on the sorted array. Steps to perform a binary search are:

- First of all, sort the array order.

- It finds the middle element of the array and compares it with the desired value. If they both are equal, it stops the search and returns the value.

- If they do not match, the control shifts to the left side and, if the number is greater than the index element, it moves to the right side of the array.

- This process continues until the desired number is found from the array.

An example: write a C++ program that has an array of 10 integers and search for a value from array. Value must be entered by the user.

```
#include <iostream.h>
#include <conio.h>
void main ()
{
clrscr ();
int abc [5] = 1, 2, 3, 4, 5, 6, 7, 8, 9, 10;
int x, y, m, s = 0, e = 9, l = -1;
cout<<" Enter a number to find "<<endl;
cin>> y;
while (s <= e)
{
m = (s + e) / 2;
if (abc [m] == x)
{
l = m;
break;
}
else if (x < abc [m])
```

```
e = m -1;
else
s = m + 1;
}
if (l == -1)
cout<<" number not found: "<<endl;
 else
cout<<" number found at index: "<<loc<<endl;
}
getch();
}
```

Output:

Enter a number to find: 6

Number found at index: 5

6.3: Sorting of Arrays

The process of arranging values in an array is called sorting. An array can be sorted into two sequences.

- Ascending Order:

In ascending order, the array elements are sorted from smallest to largest. The smallest element is stored in the first index of the array and the process continues until the largest value is stored in the last index. An example of ascending order array sorting:

Array before sorting _	29	56	24	36	87	96	71	47	40	30
Ascending order sorted an array	24	29	30	36	40	47	56	71	87	96

An example: Write a C++ program to sort an array in ascending order.

#include <iostream.h>

#include <conio.h>

void main()

{

int x, abc [10], temp, y;

clrscr();

cout<<"Enter any numbers in array: \n";

for (x=0; I <= 10; i++)

{

cin>>abc [x];

}

```
cout<<" \n Array before sorting: ";
for (y=0; y<10; y++)
{
cout<<abc [y];
}
for (x=0; x <=10; x++)
{
for (y=0; y<=10-i; y++)
{
If (abc [y] > abc [y+1])
{
temp =a [y];
a[y] = a [y+1];
a[y+1] = temp;
}
}
}
cout<<"\n numbers after sorting: ";
for (y = 0; y < 10; y++)
{
cout<<abc [y];
}
getch();
```

}

Output:

Enter any numbers in an array:

Array Before sorting:

60

80

40

90

100

20

50

30

10

70

Array after sorting: 10

20

30

40

50

60

70

80

90

100

- Descending Order:

In descending order, the array elements are sorted from the largest to smallest. The largest element is stored in the first index of the array and the process continues until the smallest value is stored in the last index. An example of descending order array sorting:

Array before sorting _	29	56	24	36	87	96	71	47	40	30
Descending order sorted an array	96	87	71	56	47	40	36	30	29	24

An example: Write a C++ program to sort an array in descending order.

#include <iostream.h>

#include <conio.h>

void main()

{

int a, abc [10], temp, b;

clrscr();

cout<<"Enter any numbers in array: \n";

```
for (a=0; a<=10; a++)
{
cin>>abc [a];
}
cout<<"\n\n Array before sorting: ";
 for (b=0; b<10; b++)
{
cout<<abc [b];
}
for (a=0; a<=10; a++)
{
for (b=0; b<=10-a; b++)
{
if (abc [b]>abc [b+1])
{
temp=abc [b];
abc [b] = abc [b+1];
abc [b+1] = temp;
}
}
}
cout<<"\n Array after sorting: ";
for (b=9; b>=0; b--)
```

```
{
cout<<abc [b];
}
getch();
}
```

Output:

Enter any numbers in an array:

Array Before sorting:

60

80

40

90

100

20

50

30

10

70

Array after sorting: 100

90

80

70

60

50

40

30

20

10

6.3.1 Selection Sort

Selection sort is a type of sorting technique. In selection sort, an element in the array is picked and placed at its desired location. Working of selection consists of the following points:

- Search the minimum value from the list.

- Swap it with the element of the first index.

- Sort the remaining values of the array excluding the first index.

An example: Write a program in C++ that inputs 5 numbers and sort them with selection sort.

#include <iostream.h>
#include <conio.h>

void main()

```
{
int a, abc [5], temp, b, m;
clrscr();
cout<<"Enter any numbers in array: \n";
for (a=0; a<=5; a++)
{
cin>>abc [a];
}
cout<<"\n\n Array before sorting: ";
 for (b=0; b<5; b++)
{
cout<<abc [b];
}
for (a=0; a<4; a++)
{
   m = a;
   for (b=a+1; b<5; b++)
   {
   If (abc [b] > abc [m])
   m = b;
if (m!=a)
{
   Temp = abc [a];
```

```
    abc [m] = temp;
}
}
cout<<" \n Sorted Array: /n ";
for (a=0; a<5; a++)
{
cout<<abc [a]<<" ";
}
getch();
}
```

Output:

Enter any numbers in array:

Array Before sorting:

60

80

40

90

100

Array after sorting: 40

60

80

90

6.3.2: Bubble Sort

It is a type of sort that is also known as an exchange sort. In a bubble, sort control visits the array multiple times and return two values on each iteration. It swaps the two neighboring values if they are not in the correct order. This process continues until we get the sorted array. Steps to define bubble sort:

- It takes two neighboring values. If the first value is greater than the second value, they both are swapped.

- Repeat this process for all the adjacent pairs and swap them if the first value is greater.

- Repeat these steps for all of the indexes except the last index.

An example: Write a C++ program that will enter five numbers in an array from the user. Sort those numbers using bubble sort.

#include <iostream.h>

#include <conio.h>

void main()

{

int a, abc [5], temp, b;

```
clrscr();
cout<<"Enter any numbers in array: \n";
for (a=0; a<=5; a++)
{
cin>>abc [a];
}
cout<<"\n\n Array before sorting: ";
 for (b=0; b<5; b++)
{
cout<<abc [b];
}
for (a=0; a<5; a++)
   for (b=0; b<4; b++)
   {
   temp = abc [b];
   abc [b] = abc [b + 1];
   abc [b + 1] = temp;
   }
cout<<" \n Sorted Array: /n ";
for (a=0; a<5; a++)
{
cout<<abc [a]<<" ";
}
```

getch();

}

Output:

Enter any numbers in array:

Array Before sorting:

20

50

30

10

70

Array after sorting: 10

20

30

50

70

6.4: Two-Dimensional Arrays

A two-dimensional array is also a table that consists of rows and columns. In a 2-D array, each element is accessed with the help of two indexes. From which one index is known as row and the other index is known as column.

The syntax for the 2-D array is:

Data_Type Identifier [Rows] [Columns];

An example of 2-D arrays are as follows:
- Int arr [3] [4];
- Char name [10] [12];
- Float area [32] [16.3];

6.4.1: Accessing Elements of 2-D Array

In a 2-D array, the array name and indexes of the rows and columns are used to access the values. For example, the following statement stores 50 in the third column of the second row in the array.

Abc [1] [2];

6.4.2: inputting data into a 2-D array

Users can enter data into 2-D by using the name and indexes of the array. For example, we want to input data from the 2-D array we will store data by following a piece of code.

Abc [0] [0] = 20;   It will store 20 at the first index of the array.

6.4.3: Initializing 2-D Arrays

Assigning values to the array at the time of declaration is called the initialization. Arrays are initialized by the following procedure.

Int abc [3] [4] = { { 10, 20, 30, 40), {50, 60, 70, 80}, {90, 100, 120, 140} };

	0	1	2	3
0	10	20	30	40
1	50	60	70	80
2	90	100	110	120

An example: Write a program in C++ to initialize a two-dimensional array.

#include <iostream.h>

#include <conio.h>

void main()

{

    clrscr();

int a, b, abc [2][3] = {10, 20, 30, 40, 50, 60};

for (a=0; a<2; a++)

{

  for (b=0; b<3; b++)

  {

  Cout<<" abc ["<<a<<"]["<<b<<"] = "<<abc [a] [b]<<:\t";

  Cout<<endl;

  }

getch();

}

Output:

Abc [0][0] = 15   abc [0][1] = 21   abc [0][2] = 9

Abc [1][0] = 84   abc [1][1] = 33   abc [1][2] = 72

6.5 Multidimensional Array

A multidimensional array is known as an array of arrays. These arrays are not limited to the two indexes. The syntax for multidimensional array is as follows:

Data_type arrayName [a] [b] ……… [n];

6.5.1: Accessing Multidimensional Array

Syntax to access the multidimensional array is as follows:

ArrayName [a] [b] …… [n];

An example:

Abc [0] [0] [0] = 5;

Abc [0] [0] [1] = 15;

Abc [0] [0] [2] = 25;

An example: Write a C++ program to declare a multidimensional array. Declare it and initialize it to store and retrieve data.

#include <iostream.h>

#include <conio.h>

void main()

```
{
clrscr();
int arr[3][4][2] = {
{
{1, 2},
{3, 4},
{5, 6},
{7, 8}
},
{
{9, 10},
{11,12},
{13,14},
{15,16}
},
{
{17,18},
{19,20},
{21,22},
{23,24}
}
};
cout<<"arr[0][0][0] = "<<arr[0][0][0]<<"\n";
```

```
cout<<"arr[0][2][1] = "<<arr[0][2][1]<<"\n";
cout<<"arr[2][3][1] = "<<arr[2][3][1]<<"\n";
getch();
}
```

Practice Exercise 4

1. Write a C++ program that inputs integer numbers in a 5*5 matrix and prints of the diagonal elements of the matrix.

2. Write a program in C++ that inputs 20 integers in an array and calculates the sum and product of that numbers. All the numbers should be input by the user.

3. Write a program that uses two different arrays to input data, like reg no and obtained marks of five students. The program should display the highest marks of all students.

4. Write a program in C++ that will input 50 numbers in an array and find prime numbers from those numbers.

5. Write a program that will enter an array of 100 values and find a number input by the user in the array. It must be implemented in a binary search.

6. Write a C++ program that will input a user-defined list of arrays and find an element from the list using a sequential search.

7. Write a program that will sort an array of 100 integers and sort them using bubble sort.

8. Write a program that will sort marks of students entered by the user by implementing selection sort.

9. Write a program that will enter an array of floating-point values and displays the greater and the smallest value of the array.

10. Write a multidimensional array that will store the following data. The first dimension will store the cost per day of an employee for the company. The second dimension will store cost per week for the employee and the last dimension will store cost per month of an employee. Display all the records after storing them in the array.

Chapter 7

Structures

A collection of multiple datatypes that can store a user-defined datatype into a single block is known as a structure. All datatypes in the structure are called elements, fields or members. These are used to combine simple datatype variables to create complex variables. The main difference between arrays and structures is that an array can only hold a similar type of data while structures can hold multiple datatypes.

The basic purpose of the structure is to create a new datatype. Programmers can create a new datatype that consists of different datatypes. In C++ programming a simple variable can only store one value at a time while the structure variable can store various datatypes at the same time.

7.1.1: Declaring a Structure

A keyword, **struct,** is used to declare the structure datatype in C++ programming language. Names and datatypes of variables in the structures are defined inside the curly brackets. It ends with a semicolon. The computer system doesn't allocate any type of memory; instead, the compiler tells a computer what type of data must be stored in the structures. The syntax for the structure is:

struct name

{

data_tpye1 identifier a;

data_tpye2 identifier b;

.

.

};

An example:

struct employee

{

Int employee_id;

Char name [20];

Float salary;

};

In the above example, an employee is the structure name that holds different types of data related to the employee, like employee id, name, salary, number, etc.; these hold integer, character and floating points values.

7.1.2: Defining a Structure Variable

This is a variable defined after the structure has been declared. Defining a structure is the same as defining a variable. After defining a variable, the compiler automatically tells the computer to allocate the memory for the structure according to its desired datatype. The syntax for defining a structure is:

struct_name identifier;

7.1.3: Accessing variables of a structure

Any data member from a structure is accessed using the dot operator. The name of the structure is written on the left side and the name of the variable is written on the right side of the dot operator. The syntax for accessing the variables of a structure is:

Struct_variable . mem_variable;

An example: write a program to provide a complete overview of structures.

#include <iostream.h>
#include <conio.h>
struct employee
{
Int employee_id;
Char name [20];
Float salary;
Char grade;

};
```
void main()
{
clrscr();
employee e;
cout<<" Enter Employee Id = :" <<endl;
cin>>e.employee_id;
cout<<" Enter Employee Name = :" <<endl;
cin>>e.name;
cout<<" Enter Employee Salary = :" <<endl;
cin>>e.salary;
cout<<" Enter Employee Grade = :" <<endl;
cin>>e.grade;
cout<<" Information you entered is = :" <<endl;
cout<<" Employee Id is = :" <<e.employee_id <<endl;
cout<<" Employee Name is = :" <<e.name <<endl;
cout<<" Employee Salary is = :" <<e.salary <<endl;
cout<<" Employee Salary is = :" <<e.grade <<endl;
getch();
}
```

Output:

Enter Employee Id =

Enter Employee Name =

Enter Employee Salary =

Enter Employee Grade =

Information you entered is:

Employee Id = 20

Employee Name = John

Employee Salary = 50,000

Employee Grade = A

7.1.4: *Initializing Structure Variables*

The process in which we assign a value to the structure variables is known as initializing structure variables. An assignment operator is used to assign values to the structure variables. The structure variable is declared on the left side of the dot operator and initialized on the right side of operator. The initialization values are written in the curly braces. The syntax for initializing a structure variable is:

struct_name identifier = {value a, value b, ... Value n};

An example: write a C++ program that initializes a structure and displays its values.

#include <iostream.h>

#include <conio.h>

struct employee

{

Int employee_id;

Char name [20];

Float salary;

Char grade;

};

void main()

{

clrscr();

employee e = {20, "John", 50,000, 'A'};

cout<<" Employee Id is = :" <<e.employee_id <<endl;

cout<<" Employee Name is = :" <<e.name <<endl;

cout<<" Employee Salary is = :" <<e.salary <<endl;

cout<<" Employee Salary is = :" <<e.grade <<endl;

getch();

}

Output:

Employee Id = 20

Employee Name = John

Employee Salary = 50,000

Employee Grade = A

7.1.5: *Assigning one structure to another structure variable*

It refers to initializing one structure by assigning it to another structure variable. It can be done by using the assignment operator. The syntax for assigning one structure by using another structure is:

employee John = {20, 50,000, 'A'};

employee Harry = John;

In the above An example, the first line identifies a structure named John. In the second line, the members of the first structure are assigned to the member of the second structure using the assignment operator.

An example: Write a program in C++ that describes a structure and stores data about an employee of a company. Use first structure to initialize the second structure and display the records on screen.

#include <iostream.h>

#include <conio.h>

struct employee

{

Int employee_id;

Char name [20];

Float salary;

Char grade;

};

void main()

```cpp
{
clrscr();
employee e = {20, "John", 50,000, 'A'};
employee b = employee;
cout<<" Enter Employee Id = :" <<endl;
cin>>e.employee_id;
cout<<" Enter Employee Name = :" <<endl;
cin>>e.name;
cout<<"Enter Employee Salary = :" <<endl;
cin>>e.salary;
cout<<"Enter Employee Grade = :" <<endl;
cin>>e.grade;
cout<<"Information you entered for first structure is = :" <<endl;
cout<<"Employee Id is = :" <<e.employee_id <<endl;
cout<<"Employee Name is = :" <<e.name <<endl;
cout<<"Employee Salary is = :" <<e.salary <<endl;
cout<<" Employee Salary is = :" <<e.grade <<endl;
cout<<" Information you entered for second structure is = :" <<endl;
cout<<" Employee Id is = :" <<b.employee_id <<endl;
cout<<" Employee Name is = :" <<b.name <<endl;
cout<<" Employee Salary is = :" <<b.salary <<endl;
cout<<" Employee Salary is = :" <<b.grade <<endl;
getch();
```

}

Output:

Enter Employee Id =

Enter Employee Name =

Enter Employee Salary =

Enter Employee Grade =

Information you entered for first structure is:

Employee Id = 20

Employee Name = John

Employee Salary = 50,000

Employee Grade = A

Information you entered for second structure is:

Employee Id = 20

Employee Name = John

Employee Salary = 50,000

Employee Grade = A

7.1.6: Array as a Member of Structure

An array can also be given as a data member to a structure. The data members can be simple variables as well as arrays.

An example:

struct employee
{
int employee_id;
int salary [5];
};

An example: Write a C++ program that will describes a structure that has an array as a data member to display the last six months' salary of an employee.

```
#include <iostream.h>
#include <conio.h>
struct employee
{
Int employee_id;
int salary;
};
void main()
{
clrscr();
employee e;
int b = 0;
cout<<" Enter Employee Id = "<<endl;
cin>>e.employee_id<<endl;
```

```
for (int a = 0; a<5; a++)
{
cout<<"Enter Employee Salary = ";
cin>>e.salary [a];
b = b + e.salary[a];
}
cout<<" Employee Id is ="<<e.employee_id<<endl;
cout<<" Total salary of employee is ="<<b<<endl;
getch();
}
```

Output:

Enter employee Id = 1

Enter salary = 50,500

Enter salary = 52,750

Enter salary = 56,500

Enter salary = 51,300

Enter salary = 50,570

Enter salary = 58,250

Total Salary of Employee is =

319,870

7.2: Array of Structures

An array is a collection of the consecutive memory locations of the same datatypes. In an array of structures, each element includes an array of the complete structure. It is used to store many records.

An example:

struct book

{

Int bookID;

Int pagecounts;

Float cost;

};

Book s [3];

S [0].bookID = 20;

S [0].pagecounts = 1000;

S [0].cost = 500;

7.2.1: *Initializing Array of Structures*

Initializing an array is referred to as storing values in the array structure at the time of declaration. The values in the array are written in the curly braces. The syntax for array initialization in a structure is:

struct book

{

Int bookID;

Int pagecounts;

Float cost;

};

Book s [3] = { {10, 1000, 500}, {20, 2000, 600}, {30, 3000, 1000}

};

An example: Write a C++ program to initialize an array of structures and display the values on the screen after initialization.

```
#include <iostream.h>
#include <conio.h>
struct employee
{
Int employee_id;
Char name [20];
Float salary;
};
void main()
{
clrscr();
employee e [3];
int a, m;
for (int a = 0; a<3; a++)
{
cout<<"Enter Employee ID = ";
```

```
cin>>e.employee_id [a];
cout<<"Enter Employee Salary = ";
cin>>e.salary [a];
cout<<"Enter Employee Name = ";
cin>>e.name [a];
}
cout<<"Record entered is = ";
for (int b = 0; b<3; b++)
{
cout<<"Employee ID = " <<e.employee_id [b]<<endl;
cout<<"Employee Salary = " <<e.salary [b]<<endl;
cout<<" Employee Name = " <<e.name [b]<<endl;
}
getch();
}
```

Output:

Enter Employee id =

Enter Employee name =

Enter employee salary =

Record entered is:

Employee Id = 1

Employee Name = John

Employee Salary = 20,000

Employee Id = 2

Employee Name = Mike

Employee Salary = 30,000

Employee Id = 3

Employee Name = Harry

Employee Salary = 40,000

Employee Id = 4

Employee Name = Joseph

Employee Salary = 50,000

7.3: Nested Structures

A structure within other structures is called a nested structure. It is created when the data members of a structure are further structures. An example of a nested structure is as follows:

struct employee

{

int employee_id;

char grade;

};

struct details

{

int salary;

char [20] name;

employee e;

};

In the above example, the structure called employee is used to store only employee IDs or grades. The other structure called details has the details about the employee, like name and salary, and it also has the nested structure employee in it.

7.3.1: *Accessing Members of Nested Structure*

The data members of a nested structure can be accessed using several dot operators. The first operator indicates the data members of the outer most structure, the second operator is used to access the data members of the inner structure and the process goes on.

An example: Write a C++ program that uses two structures salary and employee. The salary structure records the salary and grade of the employees while the employee structure records the name and employee id of the employee. It should declare the values of the structures and display the values on the screen.

#include <iostream.h>

#include <conio.h>

struct salary

{

```
float employee_salary;
char grade;
};
struct employee
{
Int employee_id;
Char name [20];
salary r;
};
void main()
{
clrscr();
employee e;
cout<< "Enter Employee ID:";
cin>> e.employee_id <<endl;
cout<< "Enter Employee Name:";
cin>> e.name [20] <<endl;
cout<< "Enter Employee Salary:";
cin>> r.employee_salary <<endl;
cout<< "Enter Employee Grade:";
cin>> r.grade <<endl;
cout<< "Employee Id = " << e.employee_id <<endl;
cout<< "Employee Name = " << e.name [20] <<endl;
```

cout<< "Employee Salary = " << r.employee_salary <<endl;

cout<< "Employee Id = " << r.grade <<endl;

getch();

}

Output:

Enter Employee id =

Enter Employee name =

Enter Employee salary =

Enter Employee Grade =

The record entered is:

Employee id = 1

Employee Name = John

Employee Salary = 20,000

Employee Grade = A

7.4: Unions

Data storage, similar to structures in specific aspects, is known as unions. The variables of different datatypes are grouped by using unions. Each data member in the union is accessed by using the dot operator. It is different from structures. A structure allocates the complete memory space required for a structure variable while the union allocates the space required by a single data member. The syntax for union is:

union name

{

member_type a member_name a;

member_type b member_name b;

member_type c member_name c;

.

.

.

};

An example: Write a C++ program that will show the implementation and working of a union. Then display the values stored by the union.

#include <iostream.h>

#include <conio.h>

union pent

{

char p_size;

int length;

int waist;

};

void main()

{

clrscr();

pent m;

cout<< "Size of union: "<< sizeof (m);

cout<< " What is Size (S/M/L)? ";

cin>> m.size <<endl;

cout<< " The size is = " << m.size <<endl;

cout<< " Length is = " << m.length <<endl;

cout<< " Waist is = " << m.waist <<endl;

getch();

}

Output:

Size of union =

What is Size)S/M/L =

The Size is = M

Length is = 38

Waist is = 32

Practice Exercise 5

1. Write a program in C++ that declares a structure datatype to store the date of birth. It takes three values and displays output on the screen the format like day/ month/ year by using structures.

2. Write a C++ program that stores the details of different cars such as, model, price, and name. it must display the record of the most costly car in the given list.

3. Write a program that enters employee's data like id, name, number, working hours, basic pay and calculates the monthly salary of the employees by using the given information.

4. Write a program in C++ that declares a structure variable and store name, roll no, class and marks of the students of a class and displays the topper of the class with the name, roll no, and marks on the screen.

5. Write a program in C++ that declares an enumeration to store the minutes in a year.

6. Write a C++ program to store a structure, bike, to store bike id, bike name, bike model and bike price. Use another structure that is declared in the first structure to store the order id, order quantity and order price entered by the user. The program must display all the values entered by the user.

Chapter 8

Functions

A named block of statements that is used to perform specific actions is known as a function. When a function is called, the clock of statements written in the function is executed. In a programming language, each function has its unique name and functionality. These are also called the building blocks of the C++ programs.

The main purpose of functions is to perform a specific type of action again and again without writing several times in the program. When the function is called inside a program control directly moves to that function and performs the task described in the block of function. After executing the function statements control moves back to the location from where it was called.

It is also called a modular way of writing programs because it uses structured programming techniques. The program is divided into several small modules or functions.

8.1.1: Advantages of a Function

Sometimes a program may need to perform a task multiple times in the execution of the program. So we use the functions to make the code short and easy. Some important advantages of functions in a programming language are:

- Easier to Code:

By using functions, it is easy to write long programs; it is easier to write a small function instead of writing a complete complex program.

- Easier to Modify:

In a program, each function has its specific name and an independent block of code. If any error occurs in the program, it is easy to check and modify the program instead of finding an error from the whole program.

- Reusability:

As we know, multiple programs can have the same function. So, functions written for a program can be used in another program to perform the specific operation. It helps the programmer not to write the same function in multiple programs again and again.

- Less Programming Time:

Functions allow reusability in multiple programs. It saves a programmer time and reduces the duration to complete a complex program.

8.2: Types of Functions in C++

There are two types of functions in the C++ programming language:

- User-defined Functions:

A type of function that is created by the user to perform a specific type of operation. They have a unique name and functionality described by the programmer.

- Built-in Functions:

The type of functions that are found in the programming language are called built-in functions. These are also known as library functions and have a pre-defined task.

8.3: User-Defined Functions

In C++ programming language user-defined function consists of the following:

- Function Declaration or Function Prototyping
- Function Definition

8.3.1: Function Declaration or Function Prototyping

The structure of the program is known as the declaration of the function. It tells the compiler about the model of the function. Declaration of a function in C++ consists of the function name, function return type, and function parameters. The syntax for the function declaration is:

Return_type Function_name (parameters);

In the above syntax, return_type shows the value type that will. be returned by the function. The name refers to the function name, that is defined by the programmer. Parameters are the special values given to a function that will be used in the execution of the program.

An example:

Void show ();

This example shows that the function didn't take any parameters or have any return type. It is just used to show output on the screen.

8.3.2: *Function Definition*

A block of statements that indicates the functionality of a function is known as a function definition. In the function definition, the programmer writes the statements that tell the compiler what to do. A function in C++ can be defined before the main () function, after the main () function, or in an individual separate file. After the function definition, it can be called anywhere in the program. In C++, a function definition consists of the following things:

- Function Header:

The first line of a function that looks exactly like the declaration is known as the function header. It is also known as a function prototype.

- Function Body:

The main part of the program that has the statements that describe the functionality of the defined function is called a function body. The body of function comes after the function header and enclosed within the curly braces.

The syntax for defining a function is:

Return_type Function_name (parameters)
{
Function statements (n);
};

8.3.3: *Function Call*

A statement that initiates a function is called a function call. When the function call statement is executed, the control moves to the location where the function is written. A function can be called anywhere in the program by its name. The function gets its parameters at the time of calling it. The function call consists of the following steps:

- When the function is called, control is moved to the destination of the function definition.

- All of the statements in the body of functions are executed on each function call.

- After the execution of the function, control moves back to the calling statement.

An example: Write a program in C++ that will declaration, definition and the calling of a function to show a message on the display screen.

#include <iostream.h>

#include <conio.h>

void print ();

void main()

{

clrscr();

print ();

getch();

}

void print ()

{

cout<< " My name is John. " <<endl;

cout<< " I'm a C++ programmer." <<endl;

};

Output:

My name is John.

I'm a C++ programmer.

8.3.4: Scope of Functions

The area in the program where the function can be accessed is known as the function scope. The declaration of the function defines the scope of the functions in a program. Functions based on the scope are as follows:

- Local Function:

The functions that can only be accessed within the function in which it is declared are known as a local functions. An example:

void main ()
{
void print ();
clrscr ();
print ();
getch()
}

- Global Function:

The functions that can be accessed anywhere in the program are known as the global functions. The global functions can be defined anywhere in and out of the program. An example:

void print ();
void main ()
{

clrscr ();

print ();

getch();

}

8.4: Passing Parameters to Functions

The values that are passed to the function that help perform the operations are called parameters. Parameters are passed to a function in simple brackets separated by commas. If a function has no parameters there will be empty brackets (). There are two types of parameters used in functions. The parameters that are used in the function declaration are known as formal parameters and the parameters that are used in the function call are called actual parameters.

8.4.1: Passing Function by Value

When the function is called by a formal parameter instead of the actual value. it is called passing a function by value. In this process, the actual value is copied into a formal parameter. The default method of a function call is passed by value.

An example: Write a program in C++ that enters a number in the main function and passes that number to a function. The function will display the 10 numbers after that.

#include <iostream.h>

```
#include <conio.h>
void tab(int a);
void main()
{
clrscr();
int a;
cout << "Enter any number = ";
cin >> a;
tab(a);
getch();
}
void tab(int a)
{
int b;
for(b = 1; b<=10; b++)
{
cout<<" The next 10 numbers are: "<< endl;
cout<< a = a +1;<< endl;
};
```

Output:

Enter any number = 5

The next 10 number is:

6

7

8

9

10

11

12

13

14

15

8.4.2: Passing a Function by Reference

When the function is called by an actual parameter instead of the formal parameters, it is called passing a function by reference. In this process, the actual value is directly given as a parameter.

An example: Write a program that enters two numbers in the main () function and passes them to a function by reference. Function should show the greater number on the screen.

#include <iostream.h>

#include <conio.h>

void max(int anda, int andb);

void main()

{

```
clrscr();
int a, b;
cout<< "Enter two numbers = ";
cin>>a<<endl;
cin>>b<<endl;
max(a, b);
getch();
}
void max(int anda, int andb)
{
if(a>b)
{
cout<<" A is greater: "<<a<< endl;
}
else
cout<<" B is greater: "<<b<< endl;
};
```

Output:

Enter two numbers = 5

7

B is greater: 7

8.4.3: Returning a Value from the Function

In programming languages, a function can only return a single value. In a function declaration, the return type determines the type of value returned by the function after its execution. A function returns a value when the return statement in the function body is executed. The return statement moves the control to the calling statement along with the value returned by the function. The syntax for a return statement is:

return value;

A function can return values in three different ways - Assignment statement, Arithmetic expression, and output string.

An example: Write a program that inputs the working hours and pay rate of a worker in the main function and passes them to a function to calculate the salary of the worker. Return the value by using **Assignment Statement.**

#include <iostream.h>

#include <conio.h>

int salary(int anda, int andb);

void main()

{

clrscr();

int a, b;

cout<< "Enter Working Hours of Worker = ";

cin>>a<<endl;

cout<< "Enter the Pay Rate of Worker = ";

cin>>b<<endl;

salary(a, b);

cout<< " Salary of the Worker is = " <<s<<endl;

getch();

}

int salary(int anda, int andb)

{

float s;

s = a*b;

return s;

};

Output:

Enter Working Hours of Worker = 5

Enter Pay Rate of Worker = 10

Salary of the Worker is = 50

An example: Write a program that inputs working hours and pay rate of a worker in the main function and passes them to a function to calculate the salary of the worker. Return the value by using **Arithmetic Expression.**

#include <iostream.h>

```
#include <conio.h>
int salary(int anda, int andb);
void main()
{
clrscr();
int a, b;
cout<< "Enter Working Hours of Worker = ";
cin>>a<<endl;
cout<< "Enter the Pay Rate of Worker = ";
cin>>b<<endl;
salary(a, b);
cout<< " Salary of the Worker is = " <<s<<endl;
getch();
}
int max(int anda, int andb)
{
return a*b;
};
```

Output:

Enter Working Hours of Worker = 5

Enter Pay Rate of Worker = 10

Salary of the Worker is = 50

An example: Write a program that inputs working hours and pay rate of a worker in the main function and passes them to a function to calculate the salary of the worker. Return the value by using **Output Statement.**

```
#include <iostream.h>
#include <conio.h>
int salary(int anda, int andb);
void main()
{
clrscr();
int a, b;
cout<< "Enter Working Hours of Worker = ";
cin>>a<<endl;
cout<< "Enter the Pay Rate of Worker = ";
cin>>b<<endl;
cout<< " Salary of the Worker is = " <<salary(a, b);
getch();
}
int salary(int anda, int andb)
{
float c;
c = a*b;
return c;
```

};

Output:

Enter Working Hours of Worker = 5

Enter Pay Rate of Worker = 10

Salary of the Worker is = 50

8.5: Functions and Arrays

In C++ programs, an array can also be passed to a function as a parameter. In passing an array to the function, only the address of the first index of the array is given to the function. It means that an array can only be passed by the reference to the function, not by the value. The syntax for passing an array to the function is:

Return_type fun_name (parameters []);

8.5.1: Function Calling with an Array

When an array is passed as a parameter to the function, it is known as function calling with an array. In this method, the name of an array is passed to the function as a parameter.

An example: Write a C++ program that will enter an array of five numbers and pass that array to the function to display the array values.

#include <iostream.h>

```
#include <conio.h>
void num(int a[]);
void main()
{
clrscr();
int n[5];
for(int b = 0; b<5; b++)
{
cout<< "Enter a Number = " <<endl;

cin>>n[b];
}
num(int a[]);
getch();
}
void num(int a[])
{
for(int c = 0; c<5; c++)
{
cout<<" Numbers are = "<<a[c]<<endl;
};
```

Output:

Enter a number = 1

Enter a number = 2

Enter a number = 3

Enter a number = 4

Enter a number = 5

Numbers are = 1

Numbers are = 2

Numbers are = 3

Numbers are = 4

Numbers are = 5

8.5.2: Two-Dimensional Array as a parameter to a Function

In C++, a two-dimensional array can also be given to a function as a parameter. A two-dimensional array is passed by the reference to the function. In passing a two-dimensional array, the second dimension is more important than the first dimension. The syntax for a two-dimensional array is:

void table(int tab[2][3]);

An example: Write a C++ program that will enter a two-dimensional array of five rows and columns and pass that array to the function to display that array values.

```cpp
#include <iostream.h>
#include <conio.h>
void num(int a[5][5]);
void main()
{
clrscr();
int n[5][5], i, j;
for(int i = 0; i<5; i++)
{
    for(int i = 0; i<5; i++)
    {
    cout<< "Enter the value for ["<<i<<"]["<<j<<"]= ";
    cin>>n[i][j];
    }
}
num(int a[5][5]);
getch();
}
void num(int a[5][5])
{
for(int i = 0; i<5; i++)
{
    for(int i = 0; i<5; i++)
```

173

```
        {
            cout<<" Numbers are = "<<a[i][j]<<endl;
        }
    }
};
```

Output:

Enter the value for [0][0] =

Enter the value for [0][1] =

Enter the value for [0][2] =

Enter the value for [0][3] =

Enter the value for [0][4] =

.

.

.

Enter the value for [4][0] =

Enter the value for [4][1] =

Enter the value for [4][2] =

Enter the value for [4][3] =

Enter the value for [4][4] =

Numbers are = 1

Numbers are = 2

Numbers are = 3

.

.

Numbers are = 24

Numbers are = 25

8.6: Passing Structure to Functions

In C++, structures can also be passed to the functions as parameters. A function can get a structure as a parameter and also can return a structure variable. In passing the structure to the function, we must define a structure before passing it to a function. Structures can be passed to a function by two methods - Passing structure by value and Passing structure by reference.

An example: Write a C++ program that defines a structure to store details about a book and pass that structure to the function to display the values on the screen. Use the pass by value method to pass the structure variable.

```
#include <iostream.h>
#include <conio.h>
struct book
{
int book_id = 2;
char name [20] = "C++ programming";
```

```cpp
float price = 500;
};
void print(book a);
void main()
{
clrscr();
book b;
print(b);
getch();
}
void print(book a)
{
cout<<" Book ID = "<<a.book_id<<endl;
cout<<" Book Name = "<<a.name[20]<<endl;
cout<<" Book price = "<<a.price<<endl;
};
```

Output:

Book ID = 2

Book Name = C++ Programming

Book Price = 500

An example: Write a C++ program that defines a structure to store details about a book and pass that structure to the function to display the values on the screen. Use the pass by reference method to pass the structure variable.

```cpp
#include <iostream.h>
#include <conio.h>
struct book
{
int book_pages = 2000;
char author [20] = "John Doe";
float price = 500;
};
void print(book anda);
void main()
{
clrscr();
book b;
print(b);
getch();
}
void print(book anda)
{
cout<<" Book Pages = "<<a.book_pages<<endl;
cout<<" Book Author = "<<a.author[20]<<endl;
cout<<" Book price = "<<a.price<<endl;
```

};

Output:

Book ID = 2000

Book Author = John Doe

Book Price = 500

8.7: Default Parameters

Default parameters refer to initialize parameters during the declaration of the function. The user does not need to pass the parameters at the time of function calling when the function has default parameters. Users can also pass the parameters at the time of the function call but the default parameters are the topmost priority in the programmer's list.

An example: Write a program in C++ that will call a function from main() function with default parameters.

#include <iostream.h>

#include <conio.h>

void print (int a = 10);

void main()

{

clrscr();

print ();

getch();

}

void print (int n)

{

cout<< " My roll no is = " <<n<<endl;

};

Output:

My roll no is = 10

8.8: Functions Overloading

The process in which the functions are declared multiple times with the same name but different parameters is known as function overloading. The parameters can be different in the type, the number of parameters, and the sequence of parameters. An example of function overloading is:

void show(int a, int b);

void show(float l, char p);

void show(long k, char z);

An example: Write a program in C++ that will call a function from main() function with default parameters.

#include <iostream.h>

```
#include <conio.h>
void print (int a);
void print (char n[20]);
void print (float price);

void main()
{
clrscr();
print (int a);
print (char n[20]);
print (float price);
getch();
}
void print (int a)
{
cout<< " Books page count = " <<n<<endl;
};
void print (char a[20])
{
cout<< " Book name = " <<a[20]<<endl;
};
void print (float price)
{
```

cout<< " Book Price = " <<price<<endl;

};

Output:

Book page count = 1000

Book name = C++ programming

Book price = 500

8.9: Recursion

Recursion is programming in which a function calls itself again and again to perform the specific operations. This technique is used to get the desired results from a function.

An example: Write a C++ program that will find the factorial of a number through recursive function.

```
#include <iostream.h>
#include <conio.h>
long int fac (int a);
void main()
{
clrscr();
cout<< " Enter a number = ";
cin>>n<<endl;
cout<< " Factorial of the number is = ";
```

```
fac (int n);
getch();
}
long int fac (int n)
{
if(n == 0)
{
return 1;
{
else
{
return n * fac(n-1);
};
```

Output:

Enter a number = 5

Factorial of the number is = 120

Practice Exercise 6

1. Write a program in C++ that gets a decimal number and converts that number into binary digits.

2. Write a program that will have a function that checks the number of zeros, even numbers, and odd numbers from an array entered by the user.

3. Write a C++ program that has a function that will generate Fibonacci numbers from 1 to the particular number entered by the user.

4. Write a program that accepts two numbers from the user. Create a function that will display the table of first number from 1 to the second number.

5. Write a program that inputs a number from the main function and pass that number to a function. The function should return the reverse of that number. Also, display the reverse number.

6. Write a program that will have a function to calculate the grade of a student by getting input from the user. Input must be total marks, obtained marks, grading criteria, and roll no of the students.

7. Write a program that inputs five numbers from the main function and pass the numbers to a function. The function should display the highest, lowest, and second highest number on the screen.

8. Write a program that will input a two-dimensional array of three columns and three rows. Values input in the array must be displayed by using a display function.

9. Write a program that will accept a structure variable that contains the details about a book fair, i.e. number of total books per category, the number of books sold per category and display the best-sold book in the fair. The structure will have 5 different categories entered by the user.

10. Write a program that has a function that will display the following output.

$$1$$

$$2\ 2$$

$$3\ 3\ 3$$

$$4\ 4\ 4\ 4$$

$$5\ 5\ 5\ 5\ 5$$

Chapter 9

Built-in Functions in C++

Functions that are available by default in the programming language are called built-in functions or library functions. Built-in functions are also known as ready-made functions and are stored in multiple header files. These functions are defined by the developer of the language and make the programming easier and fast. Different header files and the functions are given below.

9.1: The Header File 'conio.h'

The word 'conio' refers to the console input or output. This header file includes the built-in input and output functions used in the C++ programming language. Important built-in functions described in 'conio.h' are:

- **clrscr()**

This function is used to clear the output screen. When this function is executed all the content from the screen is erased. It is declared as **clrscr();**

An example:

#include <iostream.h>

#include <conio.h>

void main()

{

cout<<" I love Programming";

clrscr();

};

In the above An example, first of all, a message will be displayed on the screen that is " I love Programming ". After that when clrscr() function will be executed everything will be erased from the screen.

- **getch()**

This function is used to get input character from keyboard. The getch() function only can input a single character from keyboard. By using this function user doesn't have to press enter to go to the next line like **cin** function. It is declared as **getch();**

An example:

#include <iostream.h>

#include <conio.h>

void main()

{

int a;

cout<<" Enter any number";

a = getch();

cout<< " You entered = "<<a;

getch();

};

The above program will display a message of " Enter any number ". It uses the getch() function to get input from the user and displays the input number on the screen.

- **kbhit()**

This function is used to check whether user hits any key from keyboard or not. Kbhit() function returns zero if user doesn't hit any key and returns a non-zero value if user hits a key. It is declared as: **kbhit();**

An example:

#include <iostream.h>

#include <conio.h>

void main()

{

while(!kbhit())

cout<< " I love Programming ";

};

The above program will display a message of " I love programming " until the user stops hitting keyboard keys.

- gotoxy()

This function is used to shift the pointer to a particular location on the monitor screen. gotoxy() function moves the pointer regarding to the x-axis and y-axis. It is used when programmer have to display output on the specific part of the output screen. it is described as: **gotoxy();**

An example:

#include <iostream.h>

#include <conio.h>

void main()

{

clrscr();

gotoxy(1,50);

cout<<" I love Programming";

getch();

};

The above program will display a message of " I love Programming " at the bottom of the display screen.

9.2: The Header File 'stdio.h'

The word 'stdio' refers to the standard input or output. This header file includes the built-in input and output functions used in C++ programming language. Important built-in functions described in 'std.h' are:

- **getchar()**

This function is used to get a single character from the keyboard. The value input from the keyboard can be stored in a variable. It is declared as: **getchar();**

An example:

#include <iostream.h>
#include <conio.h>
void main()
{
cout<< " Enter any character ";
char c;
c = getchar();
cout<< " you entered = "<<c;
};

The above program will display a message of "Enter any character". The user will input a character that will be stored in a variable. After that, the character will be displayed on the screen.

- **putchar()**

This function is used to display a single character on the monitor. It is declared as: **putchar();**

An example:

#include <iostream.h>

```
#include <conio.h>
void main()
{
char c;
cout<< " Enter any character ";
cin>>c;
cout<< " you entered = ";
putchar( c );
};
```

The above program will display a message of "Enter any character". The user will input a character that will be stored in a variable. After that, the character will be displayed on the screen by using putchar() function.

- **gets()**

This function is used to get a string of characters from the keyboard. The value input from the keyboard can be stored in an array. It is declared as: **gets();**

An example:

```
#include <iostream.h>
#include <conio.h>
void main()
{
char c[20];
```

cout<< " Enter any string ";

gets(char c[20]);

};

The above program will display a message of " Enter a string ". The user will input a string of characters that will be stored in an array.

- **puts()**

This function is used to display a string of characters input from the keyboard. The value can be input from the keyboard or can display a default string constant. It is declared as: **puts();**

An example:

```
#include <iostream.h>
#include <conio.h>
void main()
{
char c[20];
cout<< " Enter any string ";
cin>> c[20];
cout<< " you entered = ";
puts( c );
getch();
};
```

The above program will display a message of " Enter any string". The user will input a string of characters that will be stored in an array. After that, the string will be displayed on the screen using puts() function.

9.3: The Header File 'ctype.h'

The word 'ctype' refers to character type functions. This header file includes the built-in function to find the types of different values used in the C++ program. Important built-in functions described in 'ctype.h' are:

- **isalnum**

    This function checks whether the value is letter or digit.

- **isalpha**

    This function checks whether the value is a letter or not.

- **iscntrl()**

    This function checks whether the value is control character or not.

- **isdigit**

    This function checks whether the value is a digit or not.

- **islower**

    This function checks whether the value is lowercase or not.

- **isupper**

    This function checks whether the value is uppercase or not.

- **isspace**

    This function checks whether the value is space character or not.

Chapter 10

Pointers

A type of variable in a programming language that is used to hold a memory address. Programmers use the reference operator to store and access the memory address of a variable from a pointer.

10.1.1: Declaring a Pointer

The declaration of a pointer is similar to the declaration of a simple variable. To differentiate between the simple variable and a pointer variable, an asterisk "*" sign is used at the time of declaration. This sign describes whether it is a variable or a pointer variable. The syntax for declaring a pointer is:

Data_type *variable;

An example: char *a;

       Int *num;

10.1.2: Initializing a pointer

The initialization of a pointer includes assigning a memory address to a variable at the time of declaration. In C++ programming language we must initialize the variables and the pointers to use that variable in program execution. Pointers can be initialized to any value, 0, or NULL. The syntax for initializing a pointer is:

Data_type *variable = andvar;

An example: char *a = 'T';

Int *num = 200;

Write a program in C++ that will initialize a pointer and display the value of a pointer by its reference.

#include <iostream.h>
#include <conio.h>
void main()
{
clrscr();
int n;
int *p = andn;
cout<< " Enter an integer value = ";
cin>>*p;
cout<< " You entered = "<<*p;
getch();

}

Output:

Enter an integer value =

You entered = 250

10.2: Operation Performed on Pointers

An operation performed on pointers works differently from the operations performed on simple variables. We only can perform two arithmetic operations on the pointers - addition or subtraction.

- **Pointer Addition:**

When addition operation is performed on pointers, it will move the pointer one step forward in the memory according to the datatype of the pointer. If the pointer variable has the character datatype it will move one byte forward in the memory. An example:

   int *ptr int;

   char *ptr Char;

- **Pointer Subtraction:**

When a subtraction operation is performed on a pointer, it will move the pointer one step backward in the memory according to the datatype of the pointer. If the pointer variable has an integer datatype, it will move two bytes backward in the memory.

10.3: Pointers with Arrays

We can also use pointers with arrays. Arrays are the consecutive memory locations with specific names and datatypes. We can also pass a pointer to an array by assigning the array name to the pointer we can store the address of the first index in the pointer. An example of array pointer is:

    int a[20];

    int *p;

    p = a;

In the above example, in the first line, we declare an array of the integer datatype. In the second, we declare a pointer of name p; in the third line we assign the name of the array to the pointer variable. We can input or access values from arrays by using pointers. Values from arrays can be accessed by using dereference operator '*'.

An example: Write a program that will input an array of five characters from a user and pass that array to the pointer. Display the last two values of the array by using pointers.

```
#include <iostream.h>
#include <conio.h>
void main()
{
clrscr();
int num[5];
```

```
int *p;
cout<< " Enter five numbers = ";
for(int i = 0; i<5; i++)
{
cin>>num[i];
}
cout<< " Last 2 Values are = " <<endl;
cout<< *p[4]<<endl;
cout<< *p[3]<<endl;
getch();
}
```

Output:

Enter fie numbers =

Last 2 values are = 5

4

10.4: An Array of Pointers

An array in which the elements on each index are the pointer variables is known as an array of pointers. An array of pointers stores the addresses of multiple pointers of same datatypes. An example of an array of pointers is:

#include <iostream.h>

```cpp
#include <conio.h>
void main()
{
clrscr();
int m, n, o, p, q, r;
int *ptr[5];
ptr[0] = andm;
ptr[1] = andn;
ptr[2] = ando;
ptr[3] = andp;
ptr[4] = andq;
cout<< " Enter five numbers = ";
cin>>m >>n >>o >>p >>q <<endl;
cout<< " You Entered = " ;
for(int i = 0; i<5; i++)
{
cout<< *ptr[i]<<endl;
}
getch();
}
```

Output:

Enter fie numbers =

20

30

40

50

60

You entered = 20

30

40

50

60

10.5: Pointers with Functions

Pointers can also be passed to the functions as parameters. When the formal parameters have defined the address of the actual pointer, they are passed to the formal parameters. Functions take the pointers as a parameter and access the value from the memory address stored in the pointers. These values are used in performing different operations.

An example: Write a program that will input two integers from user and pass them to the pointers. Use that pointers as a parameter to find the greater number.

#include <iostream.h>
#include <conio.h>

```
void greater(int *, int *);
void main()
{
clrscr();
int m, n;
cout<< " Enter two numbers = ";
cin>>m >>n <<endl;
greater(andm, andn);
getch();
}
void greater(int *a, int *b)
{
if(*a > *b)
{
cout<< " A is greater = " <<*a;
}
else
cout<< " B is greater = " <<*b;
};
```

Output:

Enter two numbers = 6
                    9
B is greater = 9

10.6: Pointers and Memory Management

Memory management refers to the allocation and deallocation of memory in a system. When a program starts the execution, the operating system sets the memory according to different requirements. Some of the important areas defined in the memory are:

- The global namespace area is used to store the global variables.

- Registers are the special memory units that built into the CPU to store special values.

- The code space area is used to store the program code.

- Stack memory is the area used to store the local variables and function parameters.

- The free store is the free area of the memory that doesn't contain any type of data.

Dynamic Variables are the variables that are declared during the execution of the program. This type of variable can be created and deleted by two different operators. Dynamic variables can be created by using the new operator and deleted by the delete operator.

An example: Write a C++ program that will allocate and deallocate the memory during the execution of the program using the new or delete operator.

```
#include <iostream.h>
#include <conio.h>
void main()
{
clrscr();
int *n;
n = new int;
cout<< " Enter an integer value = ";
cin>>*p;
cout<< " You entered = "<<*p;
delete p;
getch();  }
```

Output:

Enter an integer value =

You entered = 250

Variable is deleted after this statement.

Practice Exercise 6

1. Write a C++ program that will enter an array of 10 integers and pass that array to a pointer and sort the array with the help of pointer.

2. Write a C++ program that will input five integers and pass them to an array of pointers and find the maximum number from the array.

3. Write a program that declares structures that contains the details about an employee. Pass that structure to a pointer and assess the information from a structure with the help of pointer to calculate the gross salary of the employee.

4. Write a program that will create a dynamic array in the program to enter the marks of the students. Show the average marks of the whole class.

5. Write a program that will input two values from the user and pass them to pointers. Swap those values by using pointers and display the results on the screen.

6. Write a C++ program that will input an array of 10 numbers and pass that array to the pointer. Find the prime numbers from the array and display them on the screen.

Chapter 11

String Handling

11.1: String

The string is a collection of multiple characters enclosed in double quotation symbol. Strings can contain alphabets, digits, and special characters. In memory, strings are stored as arrays of characters which can be terminated with a null character '\0'. An examples:

"I Love Programming."

"1020304050"

11.1.1: String Declaration

In C++ programming language, when a string is declared, it is stored in an array. The syntax for a string declaration is as follows:

char array-name [length];

In the above syntax, 'int' is the datatype of which the data is stored in the array. Array-name refers to a specific name and length is the number of values that are stored in the array.

11.1.2: String Initialization

String initialization refers to assigning values at the time of declaration. The syntax for string initialization is as follows:

    char array-name [length] = value;

An example: Write a program that will initialize a string and display that string on the output screen.

#include<iostream.h>

#include<conio.h>

void main()

{

clrscr();

char st [20] = " I Love Programming. ";

cout<< " The String is: "<<st;

getch();

}

Output:

The String is: I Love Programming.

11.2: String Input

In C++ we can input a string by three methods. Those three methods are:

- **'cin'**

It is the general-purpose string input function. It only takes a string without any blank space. The values after the blank space will be ignored. The syntax for cin is:

cin>>abc;

An example: Write a C++ program that will input a string by the user using cin function.

#include <iostream.h>
#include <conio.h>
void main()
{
clrscr();
char st [20];
cout<< " Enter a String = ";
cin>>st;
cout<< " The String is: "<<st;
getch();
}

Output:

Enter a String = I Love Programming.

The String is: I

- **'cin.getline()'**

It is used to get a string including the blank spaces. Users will have to press enter to terminate the string input. The syntax for cin.getline is:

Cin.getline(string, length);

An example: Write a C++ program that will input a string by the user using cin.getline(n) function.

#include <iostream.h>

#include <conio.h>

void main()

{

clrscr();

char st [20];

cout<< " Enter a String = ";

cin.getline(st, 20);

cout<< " The String is: "<<st;

getch();

}

Output:

Enter a String = I Love Programming.

The String is: I Love Programming.

- **'cin.get()'**

It is used to input only a single character from the user. It will ignore all characters right after the first one. The syntax for the cin.get is:

cin.get(character);

An example: Write a C++ program that will input a string by the user using cin.get() function.

#include <iostream.h>
#include <conio.h>
void main()
{
clrscr();
char st;
cout<< " Enter a Character = ";
cin.get(st);
cout<< " The Character is: "<<st;
getch();
}

Output:

Enter a Character = I

The Character is: I

11.3: String Functions Header File (string.h)

In C++ programming language a header file named as 'string.h' is used to perform the string operations. Programmer must have to include the header file in the program to perform string functions. Some of the important string operations included in the header file 'string.h' are:

- **strcat()**

This function is used for the string concatenation. It copies the second string at the end of the first string. It terminates the complete string after the blank space or null character.

The syntax for strcat() is:

   strcat(s1, s2);

An example: Write a program that shows the working of strcat() function.

#include <iostream.h>

#include <conio.h>

void main()

{

clrscr();

char s1 [20], s2 [20];

cout<< " Enter first String = ";

puts(s1);

cout<< " Enter second String = ";

puts(s2);

strcat(s1, s2);

cout<< " The result is: ";

puts(s1);

getch();

}

Output:

Enter first String = I Love

Enter second String = Programming.

The result is: I Love Programming.

- **strcmp()**

This function compares two strings and generates the following results: it returns zero if both strings are equal, it returns a negative number if the first string is less than the second string and, it returns a positive value if the first string is greater than the second string. The syntax for strcmp() is:

strcmps1, s2);

An example: Write a program that shows the working of strcmp() function.

#include <iostream.h>

```
#include <conio.h>
void main()
{
clrscr();
char s1 [20], s2 [20];
int r;
cout<< " Enter first  String = ";
puts(s1);
cout<< " Enter second String = ";
puts(s2);
strcmp(s1, s2);
cout<< " The result is: ";
puts(s1);
getch(); }
```

Output:

Enter first String = 6

Enter second String = 6

The result is: 0

- **strchr()**

This function is used to check where the first character exists in the string. It returns the index number on which the character is found or returns a NULL value if it found nothing. The syntax for strchr() is:

  strchr(s, ch);

An example: Write a program that shows the working of strcat() function.

#include <iostream.h>

#include <conio.h>

void main()

{

clrscr();

char s1 [20], ch;

cout<< " Enter the String = ";

cin>>s1;

cout<< " Enter the character = ";

cin>>ch;

int res = strchr(s1, ch);

if(res == ch)

cout<< " The character is found at index: "<<andres;

else

cout<< " The character is not found. ";

getch();

}

Output:

Enter the String = I Love Programming

Enter the character=L

The character is found at index 3.

- **strcpy()**

This function is used to copy a string into another string. It will also copy the null character into the string. The syntax for strcpy() is:

    Strcpy(s1, s2);

An example: Write a program that shows the working of strcpy() function.

#include <iostream.h>
#include <conio.h>
void main()
{
clrscr();
char s1 [20], s2 [20];
cout<< " Enter first String = ";
puts(s1);

```
cout<< " Enter second String = ";
puts(s2);
strcpy(s1, s2);
cout<< " The result is: ";
puts(s1);
puts(s2);
getch();
}
```

Output:

Enter first String = My name is John.

Enter second String = I Love Programming.

The result is: My Name is John. I Love Programming.

- **strlen()**

This function is used to get the length of the input string. It returns the total number of characters including the blanks spaces. The syntax for strlen() is:

   Strlen(s1);

An example: Write a program that shows the working of strlen() function.

#include <iostream.h>
#include <conio.h>

```
void main()
{
clrscr();
char s1 [20];
cout<<" Enter the  String = ";
gets(s1);
int length = strlen(s1);
cout<<" The length of the string is: "<<length;
getch();
}
```

Output:

Enter the String = I love Programming.

The of the string is: 19

- **strrev()**

This function is used to reverse the input string. The function takes a string and returns the reversed string in the result. The syntax for strrev() is:

　Strrev(s1);

An example: Write a program that shows the working of strrev() function.

#include <iostream.h>

```
#include <conio.h>
void main()
{
clrscr();
char s1 [20];
cout<< " Enter the  String = ";
gets(s1);
cout<< " The string before reversed is =  " <<s1 <<endl;
strrev(s1);
cout<< " The string after reversed is = " <<s1 <<endl;
getch();
}
```

Output:

Enter the String =

String before reversed = I love Programming.

String after reversed = .gnimmargorP evol I

- **strlwr()**

This function changes all the characters of the string to lowercase. The syntax for strlwr() is:

　　strlwr(s);

An example: Write a program that shows the working of strlwr() function.

```
#include <iostream.h>
#include <conio.h>
void main()
{
clrscr();
char s1 [20];
cout<< " Enter the String = ";
cin>>s1;
cout<< " The string before = " <<s1 <<endl;
strlwr(s1);
cout<< " The string after = " <<s1 <<endl;

getch();
}
```

Output:

Enter the String = I LOVE PROGRAMMING

The string before = I LOVE PROGRAMMING

The string after = I love programming

- **strupr()**

This function changes all the characters of the string to uppercase. The syntax for strupr() is:

strupr(s);

An example: Write a program that shows the working of strupr() function.

```
#include <iostream.h>
#include <conio.h>
void main()
{
clrscr();
char s1 [20];
cout<< " Enter the String = ";
cin>>s1;
cout<< " The string before = " <<s1 <<endl;
strupr(s1);
cout<< " The string after = " <<s1 <<endl;

getch();
}
```

Output:

Enter the String = I LOVE PROGRAMMING

The string before = I love programming

The string after = I LOVE PROGRAMMING

Practice Exercise 7

1. Write a program in C++ that will enter a string of characters and returns the number of vowel characters from that string.

2. Write a program that will input a string and pass it to a string function to get the number of uppercase and lowercase letters.

3. Write a program that will input two strings from the user and concatenate both strings. Show the merged string on the screen.

4. Write a program that will get a string from the user and return the string length. Display the length of the string on the screen by using the functions.

5. Write a program in C++ that will accept two strings. Compare both strings and display a message on the screen whether they are equal or not.

6. Write a program that will accept a string and eliminate all blank spaces from it. After that, it will display the string without the spaces.

7. Write a C++ program that will input a string and display the string in the reverse order.

8. Write a program that will enter a string and a character from the user. Put it into a function that will find the character from the string.

9. Write a program that will accept a string and convert all the lowercase letters into the uppercase letters.

10. Write a program in C++ that will display the following string:

    I

    I L

    I Lo

    I Lov

    I Love

    I Love P

    I Love Pr

    I Love Pro

    I Love Prog

    I Love Progr

    I Love Progra

    I Love Program

    I Love Programm

    I Love Programmi

    I Love Programmin

    I Love Programming

Chapter 12

Basics of Object-Oriented Programming

12.1: Introduction

OOP is an approach of a procedural programming language in which programs are written based on individual objects. Objects are the building blocks of the program and are easy to use and maintain. In object-oriented programming, all the data and the functions performed on that data are grouped. A real-life example of OOP is that a person is considered as an object its properties are the name, age, height, color, and its functions are walking, talking and eating. Here are the names of languages developed on the object-oriented approach are:

- Java
- C++
- Simula
- Eiffel
- Smalltalk
- .Net

- Objective C
- CLOS

12.1.1: Object-Oriented Programming Features

Here are some important features of object-oriented programming listed below:

- Object-Oriented programming is based on objects. These are the main entity of the program that has data members and member function.

- Object-Oriented programming consists of a real-world scenario, which helps us to get a better idea to develop effective logic.

- Object-Oriented programming provides the feature of reusability. It means that the program written in OOP can be reused in other programs.

- Object-Oriented programming provides data hiding. The programmer can hide the confidential data of the program.

- Object-Oriented programming provides the feature of polymorphism. Which means that the object of the program can act in different ways.

12.2: Objects

Any single entity in the object-oriented programming on which the whole program is based is called an object. An object can be any real-world entity like a person, thing or idea. Objects in OOP consists of two things that are as follows:

- Characteristics are the **properties** of objects. These are also known as data members of the objects.

- Operations performed by the objects are known as **functions**. These are also called methods of an object.

As an example, if we have an object from the real-world like a cat, we can say that the properties of the cat are color, breed, legs, mouth, eyes, etc. while the functions of a cat include eating, walking, seeing, etc.

12.3: Classes in OOP

Classes can be referred to as the collection of multiple objects with the same characteristics and different methods. A class is also known as a template that describes the data members and member functions of an object. For example, a class car can be used to describe the properties and methods of car. It can also be used to define multiple objects of the car like Audi, Suzuki, Toyota, etc. All objects of cars will have the same properties and methods. While the values of the objects can be different. In classes, every individual object of the class is called an instance. In the above example ,Audi, Suzuki, Toyota are the instances of the class named 'car'.

12.3.1: Declaring a Class in C++

A keyword class is placed before the class name to declare the class in C++. It is the same as the declaration of structures in C++. All the properties and functions are defined in the body of the class. All the variables described in the body of a class are known as data members. All the functions described in the body of a class are known as a member function. The syntax for the declaration of a class is:

class name

{

Body of the class that Includes the data members and member functions.

};

An example:

class car

{

int quantity;

char name[20];

float price;

};

In the above An example, the class named only contains the data members but it can contain both data members and/or member functions.

12.3.2: Access Specifiers in Classes

Access specifiers are the predefined words that are used to allow access to the data members of a class. The programmer can only use the access specifiers within the class. Two types of access specifiers are:

- **Private**

The access specifier restricts the use of a data member within the class and is known as a private access specifier. In classes, a private access specifier is the default access specifier. If the user didn't write any specific keyword with the data members it will be private by default.

An example:

```
class car
{
Private:
char name[20];
};
```

- **Public**

The access specifier that allows the use of data members within the class as well as anywhere in the whole program is known as a public access specifier. The programmer must use the public keyword before the data members of a class to make them public.

An example:

```
class car
{
Public:
char name[20];
};
```

12.4: Creating Objects in C++

In OOP, data members and member functions can only be accessed through their objects. Objects are the keys to access the data members of a class. These are also called instances of the class. So, the creation of the objects of classes is also known as instantiation. The syntax for creating objects in C++ is:

Class-name object-name;

An example:

Car obj;

Here 'obj' is the instance of the class named car. We can access all the data members and member functions of the class by using this object.

12.4.1: Executing Member Functions of a Class

As we know, we can access all the data members and the member functions of a class by using its object. Data members in a class consist of the characteristics and member functions consist of the methods of the class. With the help of an object, we can access and execute the functions of a class. The syntax for executing member functions of a class is:

Object-name.member-function();

An example:

Car obj;

obj.start();

In the above An example, we are accessing the start function of the class 'car' by using its object or instance. The data members and member functions of a class can only be accessed by using the dot operator '.'.

An example: Write a program that will create a class and declares two data members and member functions and display the greater number on the screen.

#include <iostream.h>
#include <conio.h>
class greater
{

```
private:
int a, b;
public:
void show()
{
cout<< " Enter first number = " ;
cin>>a;
cout<< " Enter second number = " ;
cin>>b;

If(a > b)
{
cout<< " Greater number is = "<<a <<endl;
}
else
cout<< " Greater number is = "<<b <<endl;
}
void main()
{
clrscr();
greater obj;
obj.show();
getch();
```

}

Output:

Enter first number = 40

Enter second number = 60

Greater number is = 60

12.4.2: Declaring the Member Functions Outside a Class

In object-oriented programming, C++ allows us to define the members functions outside the class. A programmer can define the functions anywhere in the program by using the scope resolution operator. The syntax for describing the functions outside the class is:

Return-type class-name :: function-name(parameters)

{

Body of the member functions.

};

An example: write a program that will take two integers in the class, and define the function outside the class to find the greater number.

#include <iostream.h>

#include <conio.h>

class greater

```
{
public:
int a, b;
void show();
}
void main()
{
clrscr();
void car :: show()
{
cout<< " Enter first number = " ;
cin>>a;
cout<< " Enter second number = " ;
cin>>b;

If(a > b)
{
cout<< " Greater number is = "<<a <<endl;
}
else
cout<< " Greater number is = "<<b <<endl;
}
greater obj;
```

obj.show();

getch();

}

Output:

Enter first number = 84

Enter second number = 60

Greater number is = 84

12.5: Constructors in Classes

A constructor is a member function of a class that is, by default, executed when the instance of the class is created. Constructors do not have any return type and always of the same name as the class name. The syntax for the constructor is:

Class-name()

{

Body of the constructor.

};

An example: Write a program that will execute the constructor and display a message on the screen when the objects are created.

#include <iostream.h>

#include <conio.h>

Class msg

```
{
private:
int a;
public:
msg()
{
cout<<" Constructor is called. ";
}
};
void main()
{
msg k, l, m;
getch();
}
```

Output:

A constructor is called.

A constructor is called.

A constructor is called.

12.5.1: Parameters to Constructors

In OOP, parameters are passed to the constructors the same as passing parameters to the functions. In functions, parameters are passed at the time of function call while, in constructors the parameters are passed when object is created. The syntax for passing the parameters to constructor is:

data-type object-name(parameters);

An example: Write a C++ program that will pass parameters to the constructor of a class and perform a sum operation.

#include <iostream.h>
#include <conio.h>
Class num
{
private:
int a, b;
public:
int sum(int a, int b)
{
return a + b;
}
};
void main()
{
Num s;
Int n, m;
cout<< " Enter first number = " ;

```
cin>>n;
cout<< " Enter second number = " ;
cin>>m;
int num(n, m);
cout<< " Sum is = " <<s.sum;
getch();
}
```

Output:

Enter first number = 5

Enter second number = 10

Sum is = 15

12.5.2: Constructor Overloading in Classes

Constructor overloading refers to describing the multiple constructors with different names. Constructors must have a difference in a number of parameters, the sequence of parameters, and the type of parameters.

An example: write a program that creates a class and defines the constructor with multiple parameters.

```
#include <iostream.h>
#include <conio.h>
Class num
```

{

private:

int a, b;

};

void main()

{

Num s(120, a), p(250, b);

cout<< " Values are = " <<s.sum;

cout << "Values are = "<<p.sum;

getch();

}

Output:

Values are = 120

a

Values are = 250

b

12.6: Destructors in Classes

When the object of the class is killed, an automatic function is executed in the OOP, known as a destructor. It also has no return type and can accept parameters. A special symbol ~ is used before the destructor name. The syntax for destructor is:

~ class-name()

{

The body of destructor.

};

An example: Write a C++ program that will create a class and display when the constructor and destructors are executed.

```
#include <iostream.h>
#include <conio.h>
Class msg
{
private:
int a;
public:
msg()
{
cout<< " Constructor is called. ";
}
~ msg()
{
cout<< " Destructor is called. ";
}
};
void main()
```

{

msg k, l;

getch();

}

Output:

Constructor is called.

Destructor is called.

12.7: Friend Classes in OOP

Friend class is a type of class that can access the data members and member functions of the specified class. By default, the private data members and methods cannot be accessed outside the class. But when we define a friend class in a particular class, its data members and functions can be accessed by the friend class. For example, a class named 'C' has a friend class 'D'. It means that all the data members and member functions of class 'C' can be accessed by the class 'D'.

An example: Write a program that will create a class define its methods and members. Make another friend class and access the data members and functions of the first class.

#include <iostream.h>

#include <conio.h>

```cpp
Class msg
{
private:
int m,n;
public:
msg()
{
int m = 50;
int n = 100;
}
friend class msg1;
};
class msg1
{
public:
void pmsg(msg o)
{
cout<< " The first value is = " <<o.m <<endl;
}
void pmsg1(msg1 o)
{
cout<< " The second value is = " <<o.n <<endl;
}
```

};

void main()

{

msg o;

msg1 j;

j.pmsg(o);

j.pmsg1(o);

getch();

}

Output:

The first value is = 50

The second value is = 100

Practice Exercise 8

1. Write a program in C++ that will create a class of a real-world example. Define the data members and member functions in the class. Create an object of that class and access the data members and member functions of the class.

2. Write a class that will have the data members and three functions. Input three values from the user and display the sum, product, and average of that values with the help of an object.

3. Create a class in C++ that will have multiple constructors of different parameters. Initiate those constructors and display them on each constructor call. Also, destroy the constructors after the output and display another message.

4. Write a C++ program that will create a class named book. The class will have the following data members and functions.

    Name of the book, cost of the book, pages of the book, author name.

    Input and output functions to take input from the user and display the information on the screen.

5. Write a C++ program that will have a class of defined data members and member functions. Create a friend class and access the members and functions of the first class to perform addition, multiplication, subtraction and division operation. Also, show the results on the screen.

Chapter 13

Inheritance

13.1: Introduction

Inheritance is a programming technique in which programmers use an existing class to define a new class that inherits all the properties and functions of the main class. In this method, the class from which the new class is derived is called the base class, parent class, or superclass. The new class that is derived from a base class is called the child class or derived class.

Inheritance is the relationship between different classes that allows all child classes to share all the common characteristics of the parent class. The child class inherits all the functions of the base class but can also have their specific features except the inherited features. It is the most essential feature of OOP.

A real-world example of Inheritance is:

Let suppose we have created a class named **person**. This class has data members like height, color, name, and weight and functions such as listening, eating, sleeping, etc. All the classes derived from person class will inherit all the properties and functions of the parent class. Also, they may include some characteristics like nicknames and functions like painting, gaming, etc.

13.1.1: Advantages of inheritance

Advantages of inheritance are described below:

- By using inheritance, a programmer saves a lot of time and effort to write code for all the classes that have similar properties and methods.

- This technique allows the coder to reuse the present code in multiple cases. It means the programmer has to create a class once and can use it anywhere and any time when it's needed.

- Inheritance makes the code and programs more structured. So, it's easy for the programmer to modify or debug the program.

- It increases the reliability of a program.

13.1.2: Types of Inheritance

The two main types of inheritance are:

- **Single Inheritance**

In single inheritance, all the subclasses are inherited from one super class. All child classes inherit the data members or functions of the single super class.

- **Multiple Inheritance**

In multiple inheritance, a subclass can be derived from more than one superclasses. The inherited class will have the characteristics of both parent classes.

13.2: Declaring a Child Class

The process of declaring a child class is same as declaring the super class. The programmer just has to add the reference of the super class with the child class to inherit all the characteristics and methods of the super class. The syntax for declaring a child class is:

Class child-class : specifier super-class

{

Body of the child class.

};

An example: Write a class in C++ that will inherit a base class and access the data members or member functions to display a message on the screen.

#include <iostream.h>

#include <conio.h>

class m

{

protected:

int p;

public:

m()

{

p = 0;

}

void f()

{

P++;

}

void display()

{

Cout<< " Value is = " <<p <<endl;

}

};

Class m2 : public m

{

Public:

void b()

{

cout>> " Value is = " <<p <<endl;

}

};

void main()

{
M2 obj;
obj.display();
obj.f();
obj.display();
obj.b();
obj.display();
getch();
}

Output:

Value is = 5

Value is = 6

Value is = 4

13.3: Accessing Members and Functions of Parent Class

In inheritance, accessing the data members and member, functions is an essential issue known as accessibility. We can access the data members or functions of the base class with the help of the object of the child class. But through objected we can only access the public or protected data members or member functions. The private data members and functions cannot be accessed in the derived class.

A constructor of the base class can also be accessed in the derived class. The constructor of the base class can only be used if child class has no constructor. The syntax for accessing constructor of base class is:

An example: Write a class in C++ that will inherit a base class and access the constructor of the base class. Also, display a message on the screen.

#include <iostream.h>

#include <conio.h>

class base

{

protected:

int p;

public:

base()

{

p = 0;

}

base(int n)

{

P = n;

}

void display()

```
{
cout<< " p = " <<p <<endl;
}
};
Class child : public base
{
private:
char c;
Public:
Child() : base()
{
C = 'a';
}
child(char b, int o) : base(o)
{
Ch = a;
}
void disp()
{
cout>> " ch = " <<ch <<endl;
}
};
void main()
```

```
{
clrscr();
child obj, obj1('$', 500);
cout<< " Obj is = " <<endl ;
obj.display();
obj.disp();
cout<<endl;
cout<< " Obj1 is = " <<endl;
obj1.display();
obj1.disp();
getch();
}
```

Output:

Obj is =
    P = 0
    C = a

Obj1 is =
    P = 500
    C = $

13.4: Types of Inheritance in C++

Three types of inheritance define the access controls of a derived class to a parent class. Types of inheritance are public, protected, and private. The explanation of all these types is as follows:

- **Public Inheritance**

In this type, the derived class can access all of the public, protected, and private data members and member functions with the same access status as the base class. The syntax for public inheritance is:

Class derived-class: public base-class

{

Body of the derived class.

}

Access status of the derived class and for the object:

All **public** data members can be accessed by the derived class and the object of the derived class.

All **protected** data members can be accessed by the derived class but the object of the derived class cannot access the protected data members.

All **private** data members cannot be accessed by the derived class and the object of the derived class.

- **Protected Inheritance**

In this type, the derived class can access all of the public and protected data members and member functions of the base class. The public members in the base class become private in the child class. The syntax for public inheritance is:

Class derived-class: protected base-class

{

Body of the derived class.

}

Access status of the derived class and for the object:

All **public** data members can be accessed by the derived class and the object of the derived class.

All **protected** data members can be accessed by the derived class but, the object of the derived class cannot access the protected data members.

All **private** data members cannot be accessed by the derived class and the object of the derived class.

- **Private Inheritance**

In this type all of the public, protected, and private data members and member functions in the derived class become private. And cannot be accessed by the derived class or from the object of the derived class. The syntax for public inheritance is:

Class derived-class: private base-class

{

Body of the derived class.

}

Access status of the derived class and for the object:

All **public** data members can be accessed by the derived class and the object of the derived class.

All **protected** data members can be accessed by the derived class but, the object of the derived class cannot access the protected data members.

All **private** data members cannot be accessed by the derived class and the object of the derived class.

Practice Exercise 9

1. Write a class named as person with the data members like name, age, and address. Call a constructor and create 2 methods such as input and output to get input or to display output on the screen. Derive another class from the Person class that has the data members like phone no, height, and occupation. Get all the inputs by using the object of the derived class and display it on the screen.

2. Write a C++ program that will create two classes and describe their relationship by using public inheritance.

3. Write a C++ program that will create two classes and describe their relationship by using protected inheritance.

4. Write a C++ program that will create two classes and describe their relationship by using private inheritance.

5. Write a program that will define a class that holds personal information about a student like a name, age, and phone number. It also has two methods to take input and to display output. Create a second class that holds the academic record of the student like roll no, class, marks and grades. It also inherits the characteristics or methods of the first class. Create a third class that will inherit both of the above classes and also holds the data members like scholarship details and the criteria. Use the multilevel inheritance to show all the records and the scholarship status of a student.

Chapter 14

File Handling

14.1: Introduction to Files

The word 'File' refers to the selection of related data and records. A file can have data about an object or entity. These files can be used to store multiple types of data. After that, files are stored on secondary storage devices.

In C++ usually, the data is stored in the variables. If the programmer wants to input data from a prescribed file, it must be attached or added to the program before use. It can also be used to store the output generated by the C++ program. Moreover, a large amount of data can be stored in files instead of storing them in memory. Files are easy to update and modify. We can use one file to provide input to the several programs. It saves the typing effort and time of the programmer in giving the input.

File Handling refers to attach or add the necessary files in the program to provide input and to store output permanently. We use a standard library file or header file in C++ to handle all the operations regarding the files. That header file is known as <fstream>.

14.2: File Access Methods

It is the prescribed way of accessing the files given to the program. The file access method relies on the technique in which the data is stored in the files. Here are the types of different file access methods:

- **Random Access Method**

In the method, the data is accessed in a random format. Any data item from the file can instantly give as an input to the program. In this method, data is searched randomly and it takes less time to search the records. It is used to store a small or fixed amount of data to the files.

- **Sequential Access Method**

In the method, the data is accessed in a sequential format. In a sequential method, data is searched in sequence to get the desired records from the file. It takes a long time to search the records from long length files. For example, if we have a larger file and we want to access the record that is at the end of the file. All the records will sequentially be searched to reach at the end of the file. It is used to store a non-fixed amount of data to the files. So, each file will cover the different memory spaces on the disk.

14.3: Stream

A collection of bytes used to control the operation on the files is called stream. These streams are linked with the files to transfer them from one location to another. These streams are activated when the execution of the program started. There are two types of streams used for file handling in C++.

- **Input Stream**

Streams that are used to take standard input are known as input streams. It is used to create a connection between the program and the input file. This process is called extraction. The keyword used for the standard input in the C++ program is **cin** along with the extraction operator >>.

An example:

cin >> a;

- **Output Stream**

Streams that are used to display standard output are known as output streams. It is used to create a connection between the program and the output file. This process is called insertion. The keyword used for the standard input in the C++ program is **cout** along with the extraction operator <<.

cout << s;

Here are some pre-defined streams used in C++ are:

- **Cin**

Used to take the standard input from the keyboard. It is connected with the program and the standard input devices.

- **Cout**

Used to display the standard output on the monitor screen. It is connected with the program and the standard output devices.

- **Cerr**

Cerr is an object of the class named ostream and used to get an immediate output on the screen. It is connected with the program and the standard output devices.

- **Clog**

It is used to display output on the screen by using a buffer. The output is held in the buffer for a while and after displaying output buffer are flushed.

In C++ programming language header files and the libraries used are:

- **Ifstream**

Ifstream is a standard library file that is used to read data on the files.

- **Ofstream**

ofstream is a standard library file that is used to write data on the files.

- **Fstream**

fstream is a standard library file that is used for both to read data from files and to write data on the files.

14.4: Opening and Closing of Files in C++

In C++ programming language, a file must have to be opened before its use. We can open a file in C++ by creating an object of the streams like ofstream, Ifstream, and fstream. The syntax for opening a file in C++ is:

Open(filename, mode);

Here the filename is the file you wanted to open and the mode is the access format of that file. The access format defines the operations that can be performed on the file.

When the program execution is completed and input/output operations have been performed, the file should be closed. The function used to close the file is close(). The syntax for closing the file is:

File-name.close();

An example: write a program to read data from the files using file handling.

#include <iostream.h>
#include <conio.h>
#include <stdio.h>

```cpp
#include <fstream.h>
void main()
{
char s[50];
ofstream out( "d:\\file.txt");
ifstream in( " d:\\file.txt " );
for( int a = 0; a < 5; a++)
{
cout<< " Enter any string = ";
gets(s);
out << s <<endl;
}
out.close();
cout<< "The strings you entered are = " <<endl;
while(!in.eof())
{
in.getline(str, 100);
cout<<s<<endl;
}
In.close();
getch();
}
```

Output:

Enter any string = John Doe

Enter any string = Mike Henry

Enter any string = Steve Jobs

Enter any string = Nick Johns

Enter any string = Harry Potter

The strings you entered are =

John Doe

Mike Henry

Steve Jobs

Nick Johns

Harry Potter

Short Questions

Q: Define a computer program.

Q: Define programming language.

Q: Write down some advantages of computer programs?

Q: Define Machine language.

Q: Explain different types of programming languages?

Q: Elaborate the concept of compiling, linking and execution of a C++ program?

Q: Define preprocessor directives.

Q: Define the following terms used in the C++ programming language.
- Comments
- Bugs
- Logical Error
- Syntax Error
- Run-time Error

Q: Define Identifiers and their types.

Q: Define the following terms.
- Datatype
- Variables
- Constants
- Operators
- Type Casting

Q: Define stream and its types.

Q: Define the following.
- Standard Input
- Standard Output
- Insertion Operator
- Extraction Operator

Q: Define control structures.

Q: Define relational operators and their types.

Q: Define relational expression.

Q: Discuss the term loops. Also, elaborate different loops used in C++.

Q: What is the difference between pretest and posttest conditions?

Q: What is the difference between the counter-controlled loop and conditional loop.

Q: Define the following terms.
- Sentinel Value
- Nested Loop
- Infinite Loop

Q: Define the term array and its different types.

Q: Explain the following.
- Array manipulation
- Binary Search
- Sequential Search
- Array Sorting
- Multidimensional Array

Q: What is the structure?

Q: Differentiate the terms arrays and structures.

Q: What is Union?

Q: Differentiate between structured and unstructured programming languages.

Q: Define functions and the benefits of the functions in the C++ programming language.

Q: Define the following terms.
- Function Header
- Function Body
- Function Prototyping
- Function Call
- Reference Operator
- Pointer
- 'void' Pointer
- Dereference Operator

Q: Write down the difference between the new and delete operator.

Q: What is Object-oriented programming.

Q: Define the following terms.
- Class
- Object
- Abstraction
- Encapsulation
- Constructor
- Destructor
- Data Members
- Member Functions

Q: Differentiate between the public, protected and private data members of a class.

Q: Define the term Operator Overloading.

Q: What is inheritance in C++ programming language. Explain its different types.

Q: Define the terms.
- Polymorphism
- Abstract Class
- Virtual Function
- Function Overloading
- Function Overriding
- Template
- File Handling
- Ifstream
- Ofstream
- Fstream

Conclusion

If you have studied this book with full attention and the will to learn, congratulations! You can now understand the concepts and logics of C++ programs. You can write outstanding C++ programs and also can inspect, update and renovate complexities of programming in object-oriented approach. You can also develop system level software to shape the real-world problems into the software programs.

References

Reinders, J. (2007). *Intel threading building blocks: outfitting C++ for multi-core processor parallelism.* " O'Reilly Media, Inc.".

Abrahams, D., and Gurtovoy, A. (2004). *C++ Template Metaprogramming: Concepts, Tools, and Techniques from Boost and Beyond (C++ in Depth Series)*. Addison-Wesley Professional.

Musser, D. R., Derge, G. J., and Saini, A. (2009). *STL tutorial and reference guide: C++ programming with the standard template library*. Addison-Wesley Professional.

Kale, L. V., and Krishnan, S. (1993, September). CHARM++ : a portable concurrent object oriented system based on C++. In *OOPSLA* (Vol. 93, pp. 91-108).

Schach, S. R. (1998). *Classical and Object-Oriented Software Engineering W/Uml and C++*. McGraw-Hill, Inc.

Weinand, A., Gamma, E., and Marty, R. (1988, January). ET++— an object oriented application framework in C++. In *ACM Sigplan Notices* (Vol. 23, No. 11, pp. 46-57). ACM.

Campbell, R. H., Islam, N., Raila, D., and Madany, P. (1993). Designing and implementing 'choices': an object-oriented system in C++. *Communications of the ACM, 36*(9), 117-127.

Bodin, F., Beckman, P., Gannon, D., Gotwals, J., Narayana, S., Srinivas, S., and Winnicka, B. (1994). Sage++: An object-oriented toolkit and class library for building Fortran and C++ restructuring tools. In *In The second annual object-oriented numerics conference (OON-SKI.*

Dattatri, Kayshav, and Erich Foreword By-Gamma. *C++: effective object-oriented software construction.* Prentice Hall PTR, 1999.

Spinczyk, O., Gal, A., and Schröder-Preikschat, W. (2002, February). Aspect C++: an aspect-oriented extension to the C++ programming language. In *Proceedings of the Fortieth International Conference on Tools Pacific: Objects for internet, mobile and embedded applications* (pp. 53-60). Australian Computer Society, Inc..

Madsen, O. L., Møller-Pedersen, B., and Nygaard, K. (1993). *Object-oriented programming in the BETA programming language.* Addison-Wesley.

Folk, M. J. (2006). *File structures: An object-oriented approach with C++.* Pearson Education India.

Dubois-Pelerin, Y., and Zimmermann, T. (1993). Object-oriented finite element programming: III. An efficient implementation in C++. *Computer Methods in Applied Mechanics and Engineering, 108*(1-2), 165-183.

Lee, R. C., and Tepfenhart, W. M. (1997). *UML and C++: a practical guide to object-oriented development*. New Jersey: Prentice Hall.

Schuster, F., Tendyck, T., Liebchen, C., Davi, L., Sadeghi, A. R., and Holz, T. (2015, May). Counterfeit object-oriented programming: On the difficulty of preventing code reuse attacks in C++ applications. In *2015 IEEE Symposium on Security and Privacy* (pp. 745-762). IEEE.

Schoenberg, R. (1992). *M++, an Array Language Extension to C++*. DYAD SOFTWARE CORP RENTON WA.

Kiczales, G., Lamping, J., Mendhekar, A., Maeda, C., Lopes, C., Loingtier, J. M., and Irwin, J. (1997, June). Aspect-oriented programming. In *European conference on object-oriented programming* (pp. 220-242). Springer, Berlin, Heidelberg.

Stefik, M., and Bobrow, D. G. (1985). Object-oriented programming: Themes and variations. *AI magazine*, *6*(4), 40-40.

Musser, D. R., Derge, G. J., and Saini, A. (2009). *STL tutorial and reference guide: C++ programming with the standard template library*. Addison-Wesley Professional.

Madsen, O. L., Møller-Pedersen, B., and Nygaard, K. (1993). *Object-oriented programming in the BETA programming language*. Addison-Wesley.

Dubois-Pelerin, Y., and Zimmermann, T. (1993). Object-oriented finite element programming: III. An efficient implementation in C++. *Computer Methods in Applied Mechanics and Engineering, 108*(1-2), 165-183.

Schoenberg, R. (1992). *M++, an Array Language Extension to C++*. DYAD SOFTWARE CORP RENTON WA.

Made in the USA
San Bernardino, CA
28 December 2019